CHARMING SMALL HOTEL GUIDES

MALLORCA MENORCA & IBIZA

Charming Small Hotel Guides
Mallorca Menorca & Ibiza

Edited by
Bernd Ewert

Duncan Petersen

This first edition
conceived, designed and produced by
Duncan Petersen Publishing Ltd,
31 Ceylon Road, London W14 0PY

Copyright © Duncan Petersen Publishing Ltd 2002

All rights reserved. No reproduction, copy or transmission of this publication may be made without written permission. No paragraph of this publication may be reproduced, copied or transmitted save with written permission or in accordance with the provisions of the Copyright Act 1956 (as amended). Any person who does any unauthorized act in relation to this publication may be liable to criminal prosecution and civil claims for damages.

Editorial Director Andrew Duncan
Editor Bernd Ewert
Production Editor Nicola Davies
Art Editor Don Macpherson
Production Sarah Hinks
Maps Eugene Fleury

The author has asserted his moral right. The entries on pages 33, 37, 46 and 62 are not the work of Bernd Ewert.

Published 2002 by
Duncan Petersen Publishing Ltd,
31 Ceylon Road, London W14 0PY

Sales representation and distribution in the U.K. and Ireland by
Portfolio Books Limited
Unit 5, Perivale Industrial Park
Horsenden Lane South
Greenford, UB6 7RL
Tel: 0208 997 9000 Fax: 0208 997 9097
E-mail: sales@portfoliobooks.com

A CIP catalogue record for this book is available
from the British Library

ISBN 1-903301-22-X

Published in the USA by
Hunter Publishing Inc.,
130 Campus Drive, Edison, N.J. 08818.
Tel (732) 225 1900 Fax (732) 417 0482

For details on hundreds of other travel guides and language courses, visit
Hunter's Website at http://www.hunterpublishing.com

ISBN 1-58843-294-7

DTP by Duncan Petersen Publishing Ltd
Printed by G. Canale & C., Italy

Contents

Introduction	6-12
Reporting to the Guide	13
Hotel and restaurant location maps	14-23
Hotels	
Mallorca	25-89
Menorca	90-98
Ibiza	99-104
Restaurants	
Mallorca	106-125
Menorca	126-130
Ibiza	131-135
Indexes	
Index of hotels	136-138
Index of restaurants	138-139
Index of hotel locations	139-141
Index of restaurant locations	141-142

INTRODUCTION

IN THIS INTRODUCTORY SECTION

Our selection criteria *8*

How to find an entry *10*

Our factual information *10-12*

For first-time visitors to Europe *12*

Maps *15-25*

Hotel Vistamar near Valldemosa, see page 89.

Welcome to yet another unique new *Charming Small Hotel Guide*: to our 18 other titles covering destinations in Europe and America, we now add a guide to hotels and other places to stay on the three best-known and most visited of the Balearic Islands. It's the only guide of its kind published worldwide.

Major changes have taken place in recent years not only on Mallorca, the largest of the islands, but also on Menorca and

Ibiza. Against a background of improving economic conditions, more and more holidaymakers are seeking to distance themselves from the sort of mass tourism that has long been associated with the Balearics. And local government has set up an aid programme for hoteliers, so that old and unviable properties can be pulled down and replaced by parks or children's playgrounds. The era of large-scale hotel building seems to be in reverse, and, in its place,

beautiful and well-maintained hotels have been appearing. On Mallorca alone, there are now more than 120 so-called Agrotourism hotels.

It is this changing situation that has given us fertile ground for researching this new guide. We have found 65 hotels on Mallorca worthy of our criteria, nine on Menorca and six on Ibiza. What were previously manor houses or aristocratic estates are now almost always family-run places to stay, full of charm and individuality – perfect for our sort of guide.

As always in making our selection, we have tried to provide an interesting cross-section of hotels and other places to stay, including, of course, the ubiquitous local *fincas*. Many of these small houses are luxuriously appointed and offer every modern comfort within old walls. A few lie hidden in the mountains, others in picturesque villages and some have unspoiled views over the Mediterranean.

As usual, all the properties have been visited by our author, who lives on Mallorca. The same is true of the 30 charming restaurants which form a section of their own beginning on page 105. Including restaurants is a new departure in our regional guides. Each is hand-picked to conform with the guides' criteria: they're not all temples of gastronomy, but each is special in some way, worth a journey, and designed to give you a memorable evening or lunchtime...

Our website, charmingsmAllhotels.co.uk
Don't miss a browse through this excellent research source for places to stay in every destination covered by our hotel guides.

Our criteria

These are the same in the Balearics as anywhere else. We aim only to include those hotels that are in some way captivating; that have a distinctive atmosphere and which offer a truly personal service. While being highly selective, we also give as broad a range of recommendations as possible to suit all budgets. For a detailed summary of our selection criteria, see page 9.

In the Balearics, as elsewhere, we have found many hotels that met our criteria exactly; however, a few fall short of our ideal in some way or other, but still find a place in the guide. We hope that our descriptions of hotels make this clear. Even so, be assured that every entry in this guide deserves its place one way or another. If you think we've got it wrong, let us know (see page 13).

Charming and small

Ideally, our recommendations have less than 30 rooms, but this is not a hard and fast rule. We have included many larger hotels in this guide that nevertheless feel small because of their informal atmosphere. However, it is often only the smaller hotels that offer a truly personal welcome – that make you feel like an individual, rather than a tourist.

We think that we have a much clearer idea than other guides of what makes a hotel special; and we think we apply these criteria more consistently than other guides because we are a small and personally managed company rather than a bureaucracy. We have a small team of like-minded inspectors, thoroughly rehearsed in recognizing what we want. While we very much appreciate readers' reports (see page 13), they are not our main source of information.

Last but not least, we are completely independent: no money changes hands for an entry in any of the Charming Small Hotel Guides.

So what exactly do we look for? –

- *A peaceful, attractive setting in an interesting and picturesque position.*

- *A building that is either handsome or interesting or historic, or at least with a distinct character.*

- *Bedrooms that are well proportioned with as much character as the public rooms below.*

- *Ideally, we look for adequate space, but on a human scale: we don't go for places that rely on grandeur, or that have pretensions that could intimidate.*

- *Decorations must be harmonious and in good taste, and the furnishings and facilities comfortable and well maintained. We like to see interesting antique furniture that is there because it can be used, not simply revered.*

- *The proprietors and staff need to be dedicated and thoughtful, offering a personal welcome, without being intrusive. The guest needs to feel like an individual.*

No fear or favour
Unlike many guides, there is no payment for inclusion. The selection is made entirely independently.

How to find an entry
The hotels are organized into three major sections, one for each island covered. Within each section, the entries fall alphabetically by the place name; if several are in or near the same place, they follow in alpha order by name of hotel. The restaurant section is organized in the same way.

To locate a specific hotel, use the two indexes – of hotel names and of place names – at the end of the book. Or use the maps on pages 14-23.

How to read an entry
At the top of each page is a coloured box highlighting the name of the town or district in which the hotel is located, as well as the category of hotel. These categories generally receive no further clarification.

The fact boxes
Standard information about the hotel is gathered together at the end of each entry in a box.

Under **Tel**. appears the telephone number of the hotel, preceded by the Balearics' area code, 971, which should be used both in Spain and on the islands themselves, even for local calls. For calls from abroad, the international code 00 34 for Spain should be dialled before the 971. Following 971 is the six-digit number.

Where appropriate, **e-mail** and **website** addresses are included.

The location of the hotel, and how to find it, are described in brief. Where car parking is provided, or available, we make a note.

Often there is no house number quoted in the address, just s/n, standing for "sin numero" (without number).

Prices
We use price bands rather than figures:

€	less than 50 Euros
€€	50-100 Euros
€€€	100-150 Euros
€€€€	over 150 Euros

The price information generally includes tax and service, and ranges from the cheapest single room in the low season to the most expensive double room in the high season. Wherever possible, the price quoted is for 2002. As this, however, was not available for some hotels at the time of going to press, it may be necessary to build in the rate of inflation – it can also be the case that the hotels have generally become more expensive. Be sure to check the current rates at the time of booking. The price scale for food is as follows:

€	less than 10 Euros for three courses without wine
€€	10-25 Euros
€€€	over 25 Euros

We have only given the cost of half board for those hotels where it is obligatory. It is worth enquiring at the hotel itself about special terms, particularly for stays of two or three days or more.

Under **Rooms** we give their number and type of room, but only permanent fixtures such as bath or shower and not extras.

Under **Facilities** we list public rooms, lifts, inner courtyards, terraces, swimming pools, tennis courts, saunas, steam baths and gyms.

Credit cards
We use the following abbreviations:

AE   American Express
DC   Diners Club
MC   Mastercard (Eurocard/Access)
Visa (Barclaycard/Bank Americard/Carte Bleue)

EXCHANGE RATES
As we went to press, $1 bought 0.89 Euros and £1 bought 1.62. Euros.

Children are often welcome in Balearic hotels, but not universally. Some hotels have concerns about their valuable antiques, in others the emphasis is on peace and quiet. In some places, children are discouraged from being in the dining room during the evening; these generally serve a children's supper around 6 pm.

Disabled Some hotels provide special facilities. Dedicated rooms on the ground floor, or lifts, are specified.

FOR VISITORS FROM OUTSIDE EUROPE

First-time visitors to European countries, especially when they get to rural areas, are often surprised by the following:

- Facecloths and Kleenex tissues are not always provided as standard items.

- Private bathrooms with rooms aren't necessarily a standard feature.

- Floor numbers. What Americans call the first floor is known in Britain as the ground floor or 'O'.

- Elevators are known as lifts in Europe.

- Parking lot is a term you won't encounter. You see 'Parking' or just a 'P' sign.

REPORTING TO THE GUIDE

Please write and tell us about your experiences of small hotels, guesthouses and inns, whether good or bad, whether listed in this edition or not. As well as hotels in Mallorca, Menorca and Ibiza, we are interested in hotels in France, Spain, Italy, Austria, Germany, Switzerland and the U.S.A. We assume that reporters have no objections to our publishing their views unpaid.

Readers whose reports prove particularly helpful may be invited to join our Travellers' Panel. Members give us notice of their own travel plans; we suggest hotels that they might inspect, and help with the cost of accommodation.

The address to write to us is:

Editor, *Charming Small Hotel Guides*,
Duncan Petersen Publishing Limited,
31 Ceylon Road,
London W14 0PY.

Checklist
Please use a separate sheet of paper for each report; include your name, address and telephone number on each report.

Your reports will be received with particular pleasure if they are typed, and if they are organized under the following headings:

Name of establishment
Town or village it is in, or nearest
Full address, including postcode
Telephone number
Time and duration of visit
The building and setting
The public rooms
The bedrooms and bathrooms
Physical comfort (chairs, beds, heat, light, hot water)
Standards of maintenance and housekeeping
Atmosphere, welcome and service
Food
Value for money

We assume that in writing you have no objections to your views being published unpaid, either verbatim or in an edited version. Names of major outside contributors are acknowledged, at the editor's discretion, in the guide.

ISLANDS IN CONTEXT

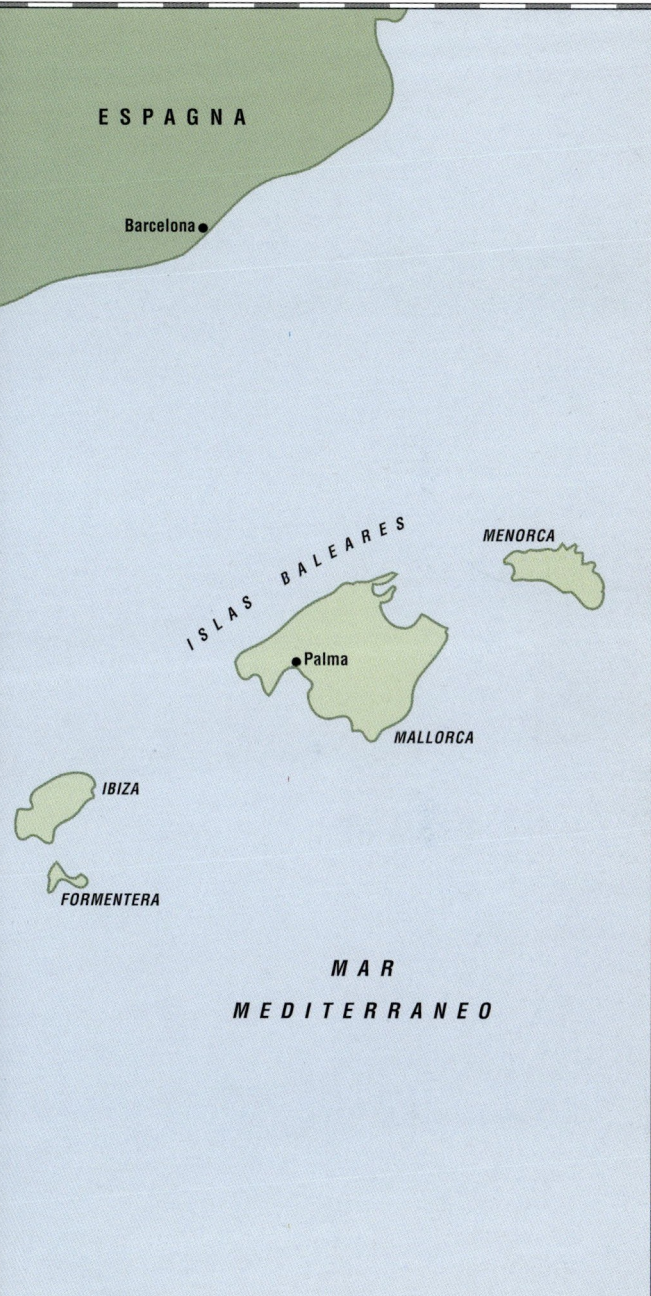

MALLORCA HOTEL LOCATIONS

MALLORCA HOTEL LOCATIONS

MALLORCA RESTAURANT LOCATIONS

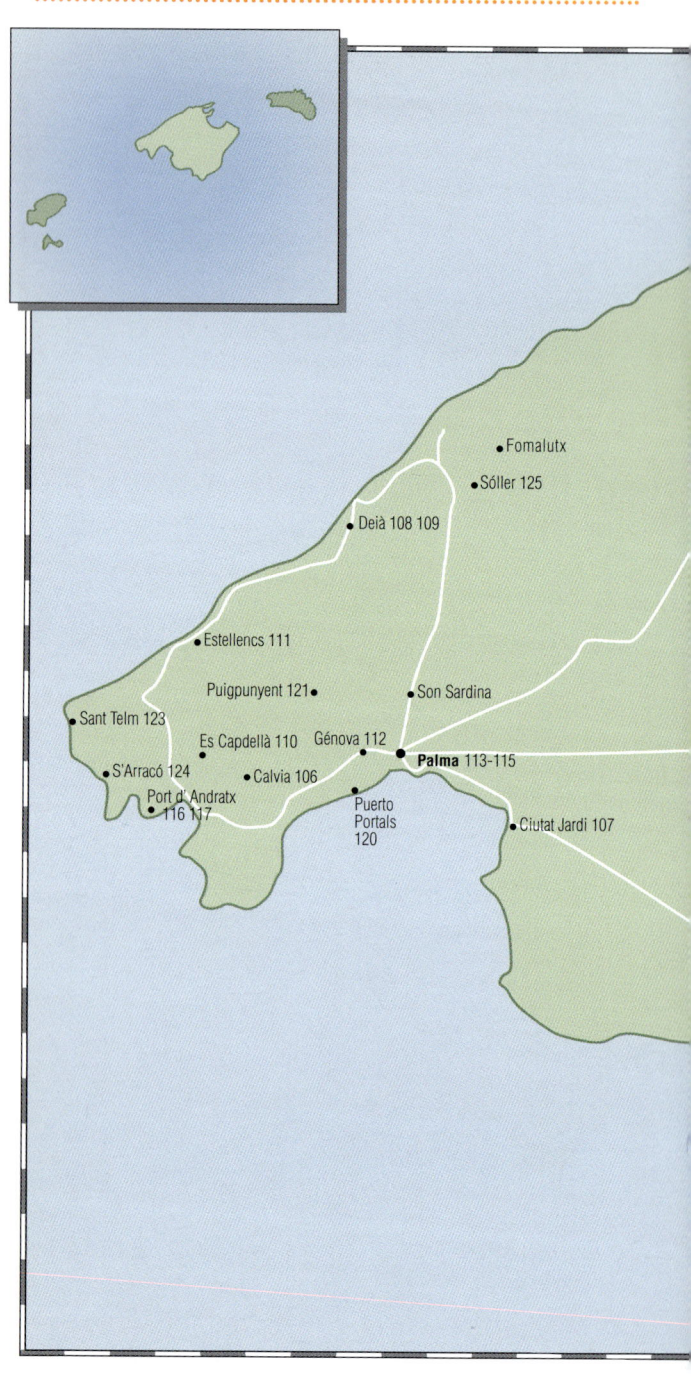

MALLORCA RESTAURANT LOCATIONS

20 MENORCA HOTEL & RESTAURANT LOCATIONS

MENORCA HOTEL & RESTAURANT LOCATIONS

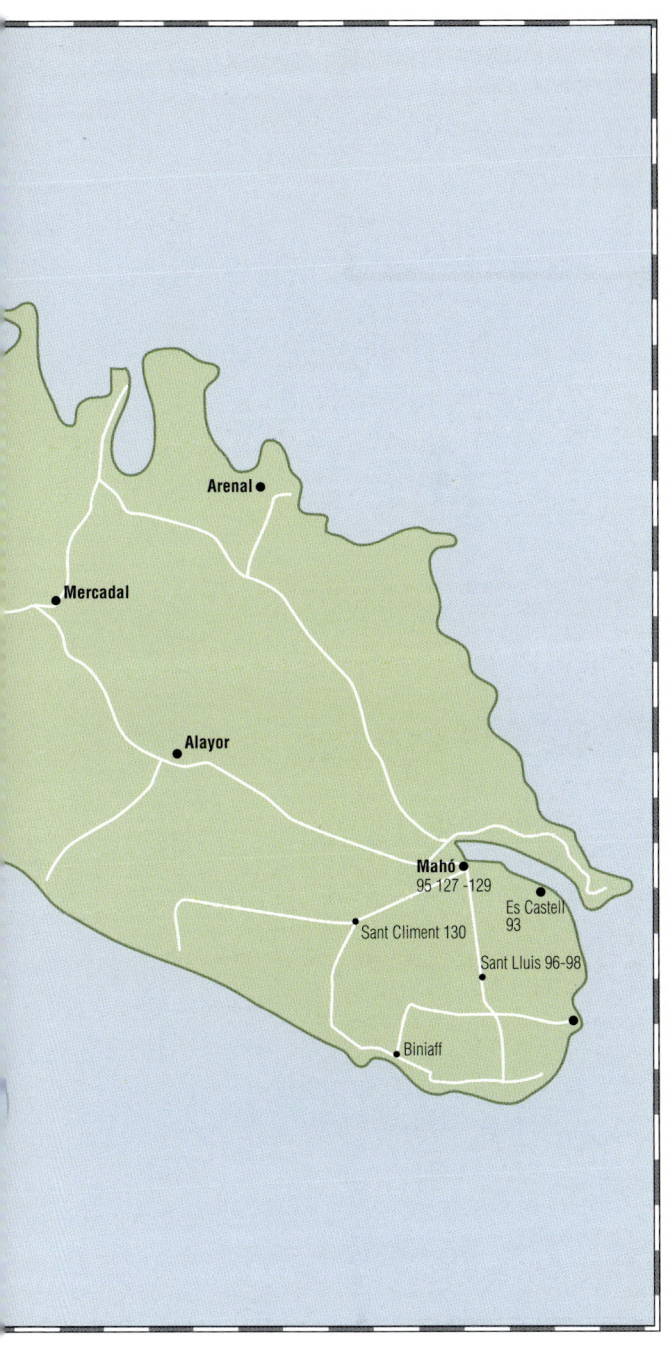

IBIZA HOTEL & RESTAURANT LOCATIONS

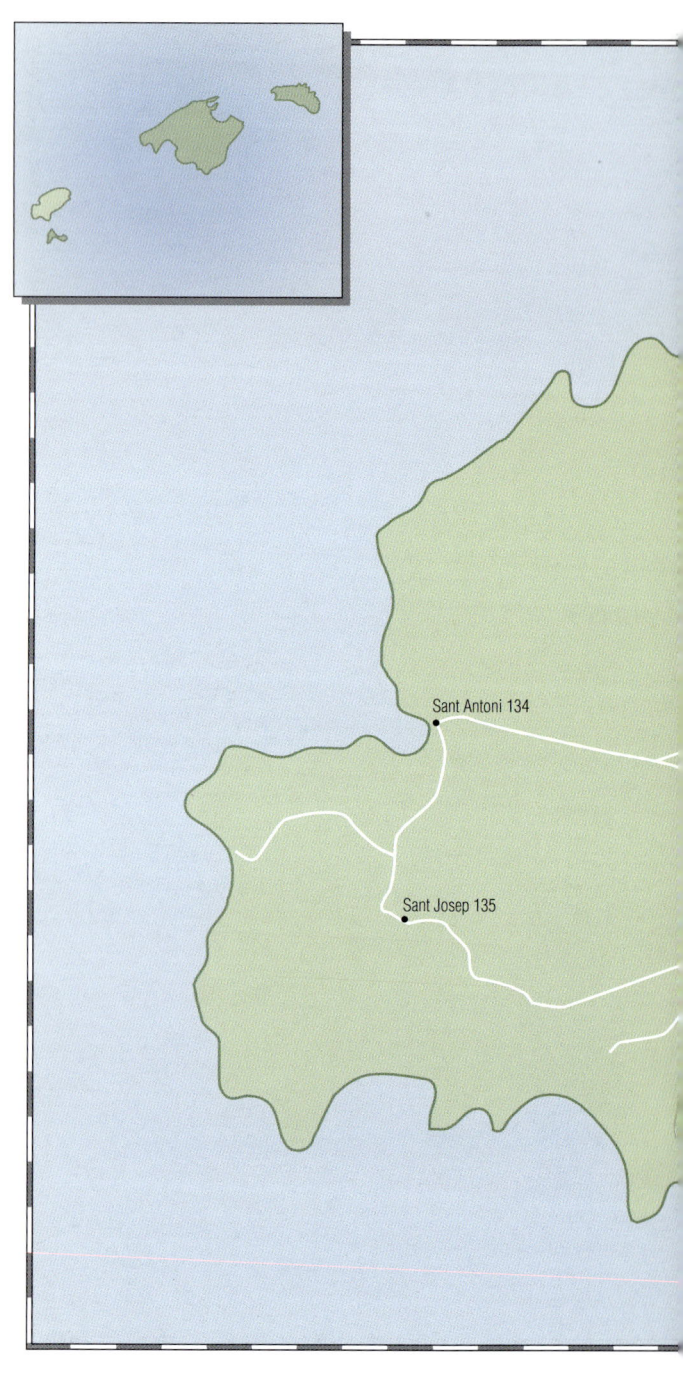

IBIZA HOTEL & RESTAURANT LOCATIONS

The Balearic Islands

INTRODUCTION

The Balearic Island Group
About 145 miles (233 km) off the south-eastern coast of Spain, this island group has a population of around a million residents - and a staggering number of visitors - up to ten million a year descending on Mallorca alone from Germany.

Over the centuries, the islands have in turn been owned by the Romans, the Vandals and the Byzantine (Moorish) Empire, and in the 18thC were fought over by the Spanish, the British and the French. They became part of Spain in 1902. See the master location map on pages 14-15.

Mallorca
This is of course the largest and best-known of the Balearic islands, a popular holiday destination with beautiful sandy beaches in the south, and towering mountains, sheer cliffs and rocky coves in the north. It's highly developed for tourism around Palma, Magalluf, Pollenca and Alcudia. Parts, in the centre and north-west, remain relatively unspoiled, but given the island's popularity as a place for retirement, and for building a second home in the sun, it's an open bet as to how long such pockets will escape the hand of the developer and the arrival of the Mercedes and BMW. The Germans in particular love this island: it's estimated that some 13 per cent of the population visits each year, or has some kind of property on the island.

Our selection of hotels on Mallorca is of course the largest of all three islands by a long way – in fact it is the best guide to accommodation on Mallorca available. It ranges from humble but charming *pensions* to expensive places with international clientèle and matching standards of service.

Menorca
This is Mallorca's smaller neighbour, and a very different sort of place. It has to some extent escaped wholesale tourist development, although there are significant pockets, and it can still claim to be (more or less) a family holiday island where you can find peace, particularly popular with the British. It has a remarkable natural harbour, Port Mahon, that penetrates deep inland, with the island's capital embracing its long creek on both sides. The south coast of the island is generally rocky with sheltered coves – many unspoiled; while the north is flatter, with broad sandy beaches.

Our selection here is thorough – we believe we've covered everything worth featuring in a guide such as this – but of course there are fewer pages devoted to it than Mallorca.

Ibiza
This is the smallest of the three, mile for mile more affected by tourism than Menorca, and it has a distinctly Moorish feel given by surviving vestiges of the 8thC occupation.

As with Menorca, our coverage of the island is comprehensive, and there are some terrific places to stay, but the number of choices are naturally limited compared with its larger neighbours.

Formentera is the fourth and smallest of the Balearics. In this first edition of the guide we have concentrated on the other three, most visited islands, but in future we hope to include places to stay on this charming island with many a deserted beach.

Eating out on the islands
See pages 105-135.

MALLORCA

ALARÓ

S'OLIVARET
~ COUNTRY HOTEL ~

Carretera Alaró-Orient km 3, 07340 Alaró
TEL 971 51 08 89 FAX 971 51 52 60
WEBSITE *todoesp.es/solivaret*

THE PICTURESQUE LITTLE TOWN OF ALARÓ, well away from the tourist throng in the Tramuntana Mountains area, is a well-kept secret largely because of its benign climate. Head out of Alaró on a narrow country road in the direction of Orient, and you enter a narrow, fenced-off and privately owned valley. After 3 km, S'Olivaret is signposted on the right. Follow this gravel road past the pool, set magnificently into the hillside. So far, so good. A short footpath (about 150 m) completes your journey.

Entering the imposing building through the hall, with its stone troughs, you make your way to the public room, a *tafona* (former oil mill), which has been beautifully restored. The millstone, together with the heavy conical grinding stone used to press the olives, makes an eye-catching centrepiece.

The rooms throughout are classily furnished, with a sprinkling of well-chosen antiques. The restaurant serves exquisite food.

~

NEARBY Alaró (3 km).
LOCATION in remote valley; own grounds, with private car parking
FOOD breakfast, lunch, dinner
PRICE €€€€, including breakfast; food €€-€€€
ROOMS 25; 23 doubles, 2 suites, all with bath, central heating, air conditioning, telephone, hairdryer, satellite TV, minibar, safe
FACILITIES restaurant, sitting rooms, bar, outdoor swimming pool, Jacuzzi, gym, sauna
CREDIT CARDS AE, MC, V
CHILDREN welcome
DISABLED no special facilities
PETS not accepted
CLOSED never
MANAGER Juan Sastre

MALLORCA

ALGAIDA

POSSESSIÓ BINICOMPRAT
~ COUNTRY HOTEL ~

Finca de Binicomprat s/n, 07210 Algaida
Tel 971 12 50 28 **Fax** 971 66 57 73

Although Binicomprat has an Algaida address, the land in which it stands is actually much closer to Montuiri, the small hilltop village on the road to Manacor. This is quite heavily forested country, but the estate has its own vineyards, which produce 30,000 bottles of wine a year. Gabriel Moragues takes pride in showing guests his wine cellars and likes to offer a sample bottle; few leave for home without at least one in their suitcase.

Rooms and apartments have a simple, Mediterranean charm. The dominant colour is white; windows are draped in white *voile*; the bedspreads are in subdued natural colours; the deeper colours of pine beams and window frames make a pleasing contrast.

There's a beautiful dining room in which dinner (Mallorcan dishes) is available on request. A large, fully equipped room is available for meetings and conferences, but does not spoil atmosphere. Take a look at the estate's simple old chapel, now no longer used for worship, but a reminder of bygone days when this type of community offered its occupants everything on the spot, for this life and the next.

~

Nearby Es Trenc's attractive beach (30 km).
Location edge of the village in own grounds; private car parking
Food breakfast, dinner on request
Price €€-€€€€, including breakfast, food €€
Rooms 9; 2 doubles, 1 suite, 6 apartments, all with bath
Facilities central heating, telephone, hairdrier, satellite TV, minibar, safe
Credit cards not accepted
Children welcome
Disabled no special facilities
Pets not accepted
Closed never
Proprietor Gabriel Oliver Moragues

MALLORCA

ANDRATX

SON ESTEVE
COUNTRY HOTEL

Camino Cas Vidals 42, 07150 Andratx
TEL 971 23 52 72 **FAX** 971 23 52 72

AN OASIS OF CALM awaits you a mere 4 km from the noise of quirky, stylish Port d'Andratx. Son Esteve, a former fortress and hundred-year-old *tafona* or oil mill, is hidden away far from the road. Today, it also houses a collection of agricultural equipment, and without losing its rustic-genteel character, the *finca* has been lovingly restored and kitted out with all modern equipment and comforts. Due care has been paid to authenticity in the decoration of the seven rooms. The beds are all cast iron, and the chairs have rush seating. The sheets are linen, and the furnishing fabrics have been manufactured to the same design, but in various colour schemes, by a small weaving mill on the island. Ceiling beams create and add a certain gnarled atmosphere and charm.

From the beautiful pool you have a view of the mountainous countryside; or, closer to hand, of the building's stone lookout towers that have served through the centuries to protect the locals from pirates.

NEARBY Andratx village (2 km); harbour (4 km); Santa Catarina vineyard (in direction of Capdellà (6km).
LOCATION between the village and harbour; own grounds and private car parking
FOOD breakfast
PRICE €€€, including breakfast
ROOMS 7 doubles, all with bath, central heating, air conditioning, telephone, satellite TV
FACILITIES outdoor swimming pool, minibar, bicycles
CREDIT CARDS not accepted
CHILDREN welcome
DISABLED no special facilities
PETS not accepted
CLOSED 7 Nov-15 Dec
PROPRIETOR Bernat Jofre i Bonet

MALLORCA

ARTÁ

CA'N MORAGUES
~ TOWN HOTEL ~

Carrer Pou Nou 12, 07570 Artá
TEL 971 82 95 09 **FAX** 971 82 95 30

ARTÁ HAS RETAINED much of its medieval character: massive walls, a fine church (on the site of an Arab mosque), narrow streets and magnificent views over a lush valley to the sea. Ca'n Moragues was carved some years ago out of the former 19thC town hall in the old part of town. Among all this old and mellow masonry, its minimalist interior makes an intriguing change to the homely, rustic style of so many of the other places to stay on Mallorca.

The heated pool is especially striking, with ultramarine roof, cadmium-yellow walls and yellow-ochre sandstone. Rooms are furnished only with what a guest would find absolutely necessary. The result is a purity which you'll either like or dislike; at least it's not predictable.

Guests can explore the hotel's 130-hectare *finca*, a 10-minute drive away.

NEARBY Cala Mesquida beach (10 km).
LOCATION in old town, own grounds and private car parking
FOOD breakfast
PRICE €€-€€€, including breakfast
ROOMS 8; 4 doubles, 4 junior suites, all with bath, central heating, air conditioning, telephone, hairdryer, satellite TV
FACILITIES sitting room, bar, outdoor swimming pool
CREDIT CARDS MC, V
CHILDREN welcome
DISABLED no special facilities
PETS not accepted
CLOSED never
PROPRIETOR Concha Morell

MALLORCA

ARTÁ

SANT SALVADOR
~ TOWN HOTEL ~

Carrer Castellet 7, 07570 Artá
TEL 971 82 95 55 **FAX** 971 82 95 98
E-MAIL info@santsalvador.com **WEBSITE** www.santsalvador.com

Sant Salvador's owners come from Cologne, and in Artá have fulfilled their dream of opening an elegant hotel somewhere in the south.

Majorcan bankers built this baronial pile around 1900. The ground plan is in the shape of a horseshoe, with galleries running around the ground and upper floors, and opening on to an inner courtyard. In all, eight luxurious bedrooms have been decorated with an individual, independent style: in one room stands a cast-iron four-poster, in another a narrow bed with a brass frame and a starry sky as its headboard. Intense, cheery colours predominate.

The Epifanio restaurant, which has nothing to fear by comparison with international hotels, basks in the popularity of guests and locals. The food, served on beautiful tableware, is outstanding, a clever fusion of light Mediterranean and Asian cuisine.

NEARBY Cala Mesquida beach (12 km).
LOCATION below the church of Sant Salvador; public parking nearby
FOOD breakfast, short mid-day menu, dinner
PRICE €€€€, including breakfast, food €€-€€€
ROOMS 8 doubles, all with bath, central heating, air conditioning, telephone, hairdryer, satellite TV, minibar
FACILITIES restaurant, sitting room, bar, outdoor swimming pool
CREDIT CARDS MC, V
CHILDREN welcome
DISABLED no special facilities
PETS not accepted
CLOSED no fixed times
PROPRIETORS Britta and Christophorus Heufken

Mallorca

Banyulbufar

Mar i Vent
~ Country hotel by the sea ~

Carrer Mayor 49, 07191 Banyulbufar
Tel 971 61 80 00 **Fax** 971 61 82 01
e-mail marivent@bitel.es **website** www.fehm.es

Mar i Vent is spectacularly sited on the coast road next to the village of Banyulbufar. The terrain drops steeply down to the sea to give stunning views, and the Vives family, who have been here for some years, have made the most of their situation: bright, airy rooms have little south-facing terraces to get the most from the heart-stopping sea views. The atmosphere is warm and friendly. In the restaurant, an *à la carte* menu offers Mallorcan country cuisine alongside an unusually interesting selection of Spanish wines. The large, kidney-shaped pool on the cliff is nothing short of an architectonic masterpiece.

Banyulbufar is originally an Arabic name, meaning 'little vineyard by the sea'. It's small, with 500 inhabitants, and perched on vineyard terraces, which have been producing wine since the Moslem occupiers first planted them well over 1,000 years ago. If you're staying at Mar i Vent, a short walk through this idyllic settlement is a must: villagers and holidaymakers alike seem peaceful and content; it's hard to believe you're on the same island as the ever-more-hectic large resorts.

~

Nearby pebble beach (500 m); Palma (25 km).
Location at entrance to village; own garden and garage car parking
Food breakfast, dinner
Price €€€, including breakfast, food €-€€
Rooms 29; 3 singles, 20 doubles, 6 junior suites, all with bath, central heating, telephone, hairdryer
Facilities restaurant, sitting rooms, outdoor swimming pool, tennis court, bicycles
Credit cards AE, MC, V
Children welcome
Disabled no special facilities
Pets not accepted
Closed Dec-Jan
Proprietors Vives family

MALLORCA

BINIBONA

C'AN FURIÓS
~ COUNTRY HOTEL ~

Cami Vell Binibona 11, 07313 Selva
TEL 971 51 57 51 **FAX** 971 87 53 66
E-MAIL canfurios@nexo.es

ON THE ROAD TO BINIBONA VIA ALARÓ, you see two mountains rising up from otherwise flat terrain. (On one of them is a convent and an estate with the Es Verger restaurant, well worth a visit on foot.) In the valley below, this country hotel has recently opened its doors. The large 16thC estate has been maintained in exemplary fashion by resident restaurateurs and is impressively equipped, aspiring to five-star status. Furnishings are aristocratic and conservative: decorated stone walls and cast-iron furniture stands confidently on oriental carpets.

In the Sa Tafoneta restaurant, amazing creations land on your table; you would be hard pressed to find food like this in any other eating place on the island; it claims to be a refined new world, *una mezcla del Mundo*.

NEARBY Alaró (8 km); Inca (10 km).
LOCATION at exit to village; garden; parking
FOOD breakfast, lunch, dinner
PRICE €€€€, without breakfast, food €€–€€€
ROOMS 7; 3 doubles, 1 junior suite, 3 suites, all with bath, central heating, air conditioning, telephone, hairdryer, satellite TV, safe
FACILITIES restaurant, sitting room, bar, outdoor swimming pool
CREDIT CARDS MC, V
CHILDREN not welcome
DISABLED no special facilities
PETS not accepted
CLOSED Jan
PROPRIETOR John Hughes

MALLORCA

BINISSALEM

SCOTT'S
~ VILLAGE HOTEL ~

Plaça de la Iglesia 12, 07350 Binissalem
TEL 971 87 01 00 **FAX** 971 87 02 67
E-MAIL *reserve@scottshotel.com* **WEBSITE** *www.scottshotel.com*

CALM SOPHISTICATION AND unobtrusive luxury are the hallmarks of the new breed of upmarket 'house' hotels in many fashionable cities; now the unspoilt Mallorcan hinterland can boast one as well. Binissalem is the wine capital of the island, a quiet Medieval town ideally situated just 20 minutes from Palma, 30 minutes from the beaches and golf clubs on both coasts and close to the island's beautiful mountains.

In keeping with the genre, a discreet brass plaque is the only sign that the elegant former merchant's house in the town's small main square is a hotel. Inside, nothing disappoints: the interior is as calm, sophisticated and unobtrusively luxurious as you could wish, special attention having been paid to the 16 bedrooms. Each is different, although they all display the same high standards, with charming fabrics, furniture. pictures and fresh flowers. The beds are top-quality handmade and feel it, with pure cotton sheets and delicious goose-down pillows (synthetic ones are on offer to those who suffer from allergies). A handful of extra bedrooms have been added recently. Breakfasts are suitably sumptuous, served in the breakfast room or on the terrace.

~

NEARBY Tramuntana mountains; Castell d'Alaró (12 km).
LOCATION main square in the town; ample parking
FOOD breakfast; light evening meals (the new Scott's Bistro is 400 m from the hotel)
PRICE €€€€, including breakfast
ROOMS 16 doubles and suites, all with bath, central heating, telephone, satellite TV and videos for rental, hairdryer
FACILITIES 4 recreation rooms, breakfast *salon*, bar/bistro, swimming pool, terraces
CREDIT CARDS MC, V **CHILDREN** over 12s welcome
DISABLED access difficult
PETS not accepted
CLOSED no fixed season, enquiry recommended

Mallorca

Buñola

Finca Barcelona
~ Country hotel ~

Predio Biniforani Nou, 07349 Buñola
Tel 971 18 05 68 **Fax** 971 18 05 68

Buñola is a stop on the Red Lightning railway line between Palma and Sóller, and as the hotel is just 1 km away, it's one you can visit without a car. (The station dates from around 1900, with an amazing façade boasting stuccoed Art Nouveau decoration.)

Barcelona, once a private country estate, lies on a hill with a view over nearby Buñola in 60 hectares of land studded with pines, olives and carobs. It is built in typical 19thC local style, the façade enlivened by an airy *loggia* on the upper level, with arches and slender pillars.

The *finca* is ideal for a large family or a group who will enjoy having the run of the place; in fact bookings are only taken for groups large enough to fill the place. Family possessions – beautiful chests, Majorcan rocking chairs and cosy wooden beds – cared for down the centuries, give it a homely feel. Paths for exploring the area begin right outside the front door. No food is served, but if you want to self-cater, there is a dining room for your use.

Nearby Buñola (1 km); Palma (15 km).
Location on the edge of the village in own grounds; private car parking
Food none
Price €€€€ for the whole house
Rooms 5; 1 single, 4 doubles, 3 baths, central heating, telephone, satellite TV
Facilities sitting room, outdoor swimming pool
Credit cards not accepted
Children welcome
Disabled no special facilities
Pets not accepted
Closed never
Proprietor Maria Franzisca Homar Pons

MALLORCA

CAIMARI

BINIBONA
~ COUNTRY HOTEL ~

Finca Binibona Parc Natural, 07314 Caimari
TEL 971 87 35 65 **FAX** 971 87 35 11
E-MAIL finca@binibona.com **WEBSITE** www.binibona.com

When THE VICENS FAMILY FOUND sheep-farming uneconomic, they created – with some help from the bank – a country hotel in their former stables. The conversion was a success, and, encouraged by this, in early 2001 Juan Vicens went the whole way, turning his family house into a luxury hotel. With a tractor, and certain amount of muscle, the younger members of the family broke up large rocks in the fields and put them to use as building materials. They believe that this new investment will pay off, and if effort has anything to do with it, so do we.

The public rooms, the covered terraces and bedrooms have been furnished with unobtrusive elegance. Bedrooms are spacious, with large terraces and beautiful baths with separate shower and whirlpool. The patio has cast-iron furniture, mosaic tables and white-upholstered chairs. In the kitchen, Santi, the youthful chef, produces superb international dishes.

NEARBY Alcudia beach (20 km); Caimari (4 km).
LOCATION signposted in Binibona – a 4-km drive into the mountains; own grounds and private car parking
FOOD breakfast, lunch, dinner
PRICE €€€€, including breakfast, food €€
ROOMS 11; 2 doubles, 9 junior suites, all with bath, central heating, air conditioning, telephone, hairdryer, satellite TV, minibar, safe
FACILITIES restaurant, sitting room, bar, outdoor swimming pool, sauna, tennis court
CREDIT CARDS MC, V
CHILDREN welcome
DISABLED 1 double room with special facilities
PETS not accepted
CLOSED never
PROPRIETOR Juan Vicens

MALLORCA

CAIMARI

ETS ABELLONS
~ COUNTRY HOTEL ~

Binibona, 07314 Caimari
Tel 971 87 50 69 **Fax** 971 87 51 43
E-mail finca@albellons.com **website** www.albellons.com

Finca Abellons' setting is breathtaking: it almost makes you feel as if you have wings. From the outsize terrace, with its beautiful swimming pool, you have a stunning view to Capo Farrutx.

Formerly an estate of the Vicens family, they now run it as a country hotel. The whole family is involved in looking after the guests, who want for nothing. No expense has been spared in renovating the house, very tastefully, in the typical Majorcan country house style. The design of the rooms varies. Here you sleep under a canopy, there in an antique four-poster covered with a fine hand-embroidered bedspread. All the rooms have a sound system and satellite TV. The bathrooms are very comfortable and are fitted with tubs.

Lovers of country cooking will appreciate the food, and are even allowed into the kitchen to lift the lids off pots.

The garden, with its dense stands of carobs and pines, makes a great place in which to mellow out, or socialize.

Nearby Caimari (4 km).
Location at exit of Binibona in own grounds; private car parking
Food breakfast, dinner
Price €€€-€€€€, including breakfast, food @@
Rooms 16; 12 doubles, 1 junior suite, 3 suites, all with bath, central heating, air conditioning, telephone, hairdryer, satellite TV, minibar
Facilities restaurant, sitting room, bar, outdoor swimming pool, Jacuzzi
Credit cards AE, MC, V
Children welcome
Disabled no special facilities
Pets not accepted
Closed never
Proprietor Sebastian Vicens

MALLORCA

CALA FORNELLS-PEGUERA

PETIT CALA FORNELLS
~ COUNTRY HOTEL ~

Carrer Playas Fornells, 07160 Peguera
Tel 971 68 54 05 **Fax** 971 68 54 43
e-mail petitcf@baleares.com

This is a 1970s development designed by German-Russian architect Pedro Otzoup, from Port d'Andratx. The large complex, consisting of modular, earth-coloured houses with contrasting white balustrades, was inspired by similar places on Ibiza.

Actually, Cala Fornells is part of Peguera, but, sitting on its hill, it is somewhat apart from the hustle and bustle of the Peguera beaches, making it pleasantly private by comparison.

The bedrooms are not particularly big, so if you can, take a junior suite: these are more spacious and newly decorated in the latest country house style. (Size of bath here is a price barometer: the more you pay, the bigger the tub.)

The hotel terraces look directly down on to Peguera's expansive bay and here you can sunbathe in peace; there's even some natural shade from the pine trees. A small sauna, a Turkish bath, a gym, an indoor pool and huge outdoor pool will keep you busy in between. A feel-good hotel for guests who like Peguera, but want a more exclusive ambience.

~

Nearby Peguera (1.5 km), beach (500 m).
Location above the Fornells bay; own grounds and private car parking
Food breakfast, lunch, dinner
Price €€€-€€€€, including breakfast, food @@
Rooms 24; 12 doubles, 12 junior suites, all with bath, central heating, air conditioning, telephone, hairdryer, satellite TV, minibar, safe
Facilities restaurants, sitting rooms, bar, outdoor swimming pool, indoor swimming pool, sauna, Turkish bath, gym, massage on request
Credit cards AE, MC, V
Children welcome
Disabled no special facilities
Pets dogs up to 15 kg accepted **Closed** 4 Nov-21 Dec
Manager Diego Gonzalvo

Mallorca

Cala Rajada

Hotel Ses Rotges
~ Village Inn ~

Rafael Blanes 21, 07590 Cala Rajada
Tel 971 56 31 08 **Fax** 971 56 43 45

Some years ago it might have been a surprise to find a well-established French-run hotel in the middle of this village on Mallorca's east coast. Today, it would come as no surprise at all – Cala Rajada is now a lively, cosmopolitan holiday town. The Tétards have kept pace with the local development, cleverly extending their pink-stone hotel in the same style as the original buildings, with arched windows and wrought-iron balconies.

The hotel, on the corner of two quiet streets near the beach, overlooks a quiet internal courtyard – a wonderful place in which to relax among trailing plants and colourful flowers. The popular restaurant adjoins the courtyard and is set with red and white tables under a beamed roof. In winter, dinner is served inside in another large, cheerful room. The oldest part of the building, around the original chimney, is now a cosy sitting room. The bedrooms are spacious and airy; they are supposed to be individually furnished, but the ones we saw all had the same tiled floors, wooden furniture and bedheads, star-shaped mirrors and modern bathrooms. Food is a highlight, earning one of the island's few Michelin stars.

Nearby Artá and monastery (10 km).
Location 200 m from the beach
Food breakfast, lunch, dinner
Price €€€-€€€€, breakfast €€, other meals €€-€€€
Rooms 24; 18 doubles, 2 singles, 1 family room, 3 suites, all with bath, central heating, air conditioning, telephone, satellite TV, safe
Facilities bar, restaurant, sitting room with fireplace, TV room, patio
Credit cards AE, DC, MC, V
Children welcome
Disabled access difficult
Pets not accepted
Closed end Nov-1 Mar
Proprietor Gérard Charles Tétard

MALLORCA

CALA SANT VICENT

HOTEL NIU
~ SEASIDE HOTEL ~

Cala Barques s/n Cala Sant Vincent
TEL 971 53 01 00 **FAX** 971 53 12 20
E-MAIL *hotel-niu@retemail.es*

UP HERE IN THE NORTH OF THE ISLAND, on the fringes of the Tramuntana mountains, tourism has always had a different face from elsewhere on Mallorca – and perhaps especially from the south-west. As early as the 1950s, the English were coming to this corner. They found it suited their idea of a family holiday, and the little bay of Cala Sant Vicent, with the Hotel Niu, fit the niche exactly. From outside, the hotel looks a little unkempt: but put that down to its exposed seaside position.

Inside, you'll find all in good order. The bar, and the beautiful sitting room giving on to the terrace, are furnished in Ibizan style, with pretty cane furniture, tables fashioned from white plaster pedestals, and upholstered stone benches. The rooms have quite grand cast-iron canopied beds and pleasing sisal carpets. Not all have sea views, so specify this when booking. The food is good, plain Mallorcan fare. Hotel staff are very attentive, but sometimes the service is rather stretched; when the pressure is on, some of them can be less sunny than usual.

~

NEARBY Puerto Pollença (12 km).
LOCATION own grounds and private car parking
FOOD breakfast, lunch, dinner
PRICE rooms €€-€€€, including breakfast, food €-€€
ROOMS 27; 1 single, 23 doubles, 3 suites, all with bath, central heating, air conditioning, telephone, hairdryer, satellite TV, minibar
FACILITIES 2 restaurants, sitting room, bar
CREDIT CARDS AE, MC, V
CHILDREN welcome
DISABLED no special facilities
PETS not accepted **CLOSED** never
MANAGER Isabel Fluxa Torres

MALLORCA

CALVIA

MOFARÉS
~ COUNTRY HOTEL ~

Carretera Calvia-Capdellá, km 1, 07184 Calvia
Tel 971 67 02 42 **Fax** 971 67 00 71

Leaving Calvia on the road for Capdellá, directly opposite Calvia's sports complex, lies the estate of Mofarés, dating back to the 13th century. Much of its principal building, the manor house, with its broad façade, is built in the architectural style of that period. Inside, you'll find rooms arranged, again in medieval style, not one behind the other but next to each other.

Owner Antonio Rotger was one of those quick to sense the changes afoot on Mallorca. Although he still owns 130 hectares of land, he took the risk of abandoning labour-intensive (and not particularly lucrative) farming in favour of turning his house into a hotel. He seems to have made the right decision: the place, and the owner, have adapted well to their new life.

The historic fountain on the patio, the immense olive press and the old kitchen are just a few of the place's attractive features. The rooms, in rustic style, some with canopied beds and antique furniture, are comfortable and friendly. The cosy breakfast room makes a wonderful start to the day. For water rats, there is a secluded swimming pool. The excursions to the mountain villages of Puigpunyent and Galilea are highly recommended.

~

Nearby Santa Catarina vineyard (Capdellá-Andratx road, 8 km)
Location on Es Capdellá road, opposite the sports complex; own grounds and private car parking
Food breakfast
Price €€€-€€€€, including breakfast
Rooms 11 doubles, all with bath, central heating, air conditioning, telephone, hairdryer, satellite TV, minibar
Facilities swimming pool
Credit cards not accepted **Children** welcome **Disabled** no special facilities **Pets** not accepted
Closed never
Proprietor Antonio Rotger

Mallorca

Calvia

Son Malero
~ Country hotel ~

Camino Son Malero s/n, 07184 Calvia
Tel 971 67 03 01 **Fax** 971 67 03 01

Calvia, formerly a modest village in the south-west of Mallorca, has become one of the wealthiest districts of Spain, thanks to the rise of towns along the coast from Ilettes to Peguera. Local government is investing a large part of its income upgrading resorts developed for the most part in the 1960s and 1970s. Nonetheless, Calvia still offers its visitors a glimpse of peaceful, everyday Mallorcan life as it used to be.

Gabriel Clar has been running Son Malero since 1995 as a charming country-style hotel, decorated with wonderful old objects. The rooms have rustic charm, and all modern conveniences. The swimming pool is large. A barbecue, and the old wine cellar, are at guests' disposal: should you want to organize your own barbecue with friends, the owners will be only too pleased.

The hotel stands next to Calvia's town hall, a triumphant modern sandstone building, and a symbol of spiralling tax revenues.

~

Nearby Galilea, a small mountain village to the north-west (9 km); Palma Nova beach (8 km).
Location 1 km from the centre of the village in own grounds with private car parking
Food breakfast
Price €€€ including breakfast
Rooms 6; 4 doubles, 1 apartment, 1 studio, all with bath, central heating, minibar, satellite TV
Facilities outdoor swimming pool, gym, bicycles
Credit cards not accepted
Children welcome
Disabled access difficult
Pets not accepted
Closed never
Proprietor Gabriel Clar

Mallorca

Campanet

Monnaber Nou
~ Country hotel ~

Possessió de Monnaber Nou, 07310 Campanet
Tel 971 87 71 76 **Fax** 971 87 71 27
E-MAIL *monnaber@fehm.es* **WEBSITE** *www.fehm.es/hoteles/monnaber*

THIS OLD COUNTRY ESTATE LIES AT THE FOOT of the Tramuntana mountains, in about 1.5 square kilometres. Mallorca's luxuriant vegetation has taken a hold here, with an abundance of ancient olive, almond and carob trees.

In the main living room, the *tafona* (oil mill) captivates guests with its black millstone, as does the upper mahogany gallery with its beautiful rounded arches. The congenial atmosphere extends to the bedrooms, which have wonderful old olivewood exposed beams, stone walls and antique furnture. The curtain material is multicoloured local fabric with geometric designs. Bathrooms are handsome and generously proportioned.

The restaurant provides first-rate cooking, which can be enjoyed on the covered terrace, with its commanding views. The extensive grounds have two outdoor pools and two tennis courts; they're big enough for everyone to find a peaceful spot in which to relax.

NEARBY Campanet (2 km); Alcudia beach (15 km).
LOCATION at the exit to the town in own grounds with private parking
FOOD breakfast, lunch, dinner
PRICE €€€-€€€€, incuding breakfast, food €€-€€€
ROOMS 22; 8 doubles, 6 junior suites, 8 apartments, all with bath, central heating, air conditioning, telephone, hairdryer, satellite TV, minibar, safe
FACILITIES restaurant, sitting rooms, bar, 2 outdoor pools, 2 tennis courts, beauty salon, gym, 2 saunas, steam bath, massage, Jacuzzi
CREDIT CARDS AE, MC, V
CHILDREN welcome
DISABLED no special facilities
PETS not accepted
CLOSED never
MANAGER Eulogio Nicolau

MALLORCA

CAMPOS

SANT BLAI
~ COUNTRY HOTEL ~

Carreterra Campos-Sant Jordi, km 2, 07630 Campas
TEL 971 65 05 67 **FAX** 971 65 05 67
E-MAIL agrotourismo@santblai.com

HERE IS A CLASSIC CHARMING SMALL HOTEL: guests feel as if they are staying with friends in the country. Not too long ago, cows were kept here, and there was a not particularly profitable dairy.

The furnishings are restricted to what is absolutely necessary in a farmhouse: your room will have a bed with fine white linen, a chair or two and a table. The walls are of beige, square-cut stone. Breakfast is a light buffet with fresh produce from neighbouring farms: cheese, eggs, milk, homebaked bread and jams. A little observatory has also been built here for stargazing on the many clear nights. For hot days, there is a beautiful swimming pool near the old mill. Sant Blai could well be the farm holiday of your dreams. And the beautiful beach of Es Trenc is minutes away by car.

NEARBY Campos (3 km); Es Trenc (6 km).
LOCATION south side of the village, signposted, in own grounds with private car parking
FOOD breakfast, other meals on request
PRICE ©©, including breakfast
ROOMS 4; 2 doubles, 1 junior suite, 1 suite, all with bath, central heating, air conditioning, satellite TV (in the recreation room)
FACILITIES sitting room with TV, restaurant, outdoor swimming pool
CREDIT CARDS not accepted
CHILDREN welcome
DISABLED no special facilities
PETS not accepted
CLOSED never
MANAGER Monica Glez Court

Mallorca

Campos

Son Bernadinet
~ Country hotel ~

Carretera Porreres-Campos, km 6.9, 07630 Campos
Tel 971 18 16 50 **Fax** 971 18 60 43

Campos is a modest village, whose inhabitants manage as best as they can through farming. But it has the rights to the most beautiful beach in the area, Es Trenc, where you can hire beach huts, loungers and parasols – in other words, it's unspoiled by noisy watersports – though, of course, not everyone will see that as a bonus.

The Fernandez family forsook farming for tourism in 1996, converting their wonderful *finca* into a country hotel. The main building accommodates three cosy *salons* and the dining room with its open fireplace. The generously proportioned, rustic bedrooms are fitted out with modern designer furniture and all have a terrace. Baths are equipped with hydromassage. Guests get together for sociable evenings around the large swimming pool with its barbecue area.

Nearby Campos (3 km).
Location outside village in own grounds with private car parking
Food breakfast; lunch and dinner on request
Price €€€€, including breakfast, food €€
Rooms 11; 6 doubles, 1 suite, 4 junior suites, all with bath, central heating, air conditioning, telephone, hairdryer, satellite TV, minibar
Facilities dining room, sitting rooms, outdoor swimming pool, bicycles
Credit cards MC, V
Children welcome
Disabled no special facilities
Pets not accepted
Closed Dec
Manager Alicia Fernandez

MALLORCA

CA'S CONCOS

SA GALERA
~ COUNTRY HOTEL ~

Carretera Santanyi-Ca's Concos, km 6.3, Ca's Concos
TEL 971 84 20 70 **FAX** 971 18 37 47

Ca's Concos is a sleepy, delectable little village with a church, two or three bars and an outstanding restaurant, the Viena, owned by Rainer Fichel from Hamburg. Sa Galera, a former 17thC manor house, is another of its assets. It has been comprehensively restored, but without losing its original character. The rooms are tastefully furnished in country-house style; cosy groups of cane chairs are dotted about the ground floor, inviting you to pause. Bathrooms are in country style with good use of contrasting tile colours. Paintings by local artists are hung throughout the hotel, including some by locally recognized names such as Bernardi Roig, Pep Coll and Antonio Salamanca. The food is unpretentious but excellent, based on the freshest of ingredients.

Although the hotel is in Mallorca's fertile south-east corner, it's curious that not much farming goes on hereabouts.

NEARBY Santanyi (6 km).
LOCATION at the edge of the village in own grounds, with private car parking
FOOD breakfast, dinner
PRICE rooms €€€, studio €€€€r, including breakfast; food €€
ROOMS 18; 17 doubles, 1 apartment, all with bath, central heating, air conditioning, telephone, hairdryer, satellite TV, minibar
FACILITIES restaurant, *salon*, bar, outdoor swimming pool
CREDIT CARDS MC, V
CHILDREN welcome
DISABLED no special facilities
PETS not accepted
CLOSED never
PROPRIETOR Simon Bonet

MALLORCA

COSTITX

SON PORRÓ
~ COUNTRY HOTEL ~

Diseminados, Poligno 3° Parcela 223, Costitx
Tel 971 18 20 13 **Fax** 971 18 20 12

THE OBVIOUS WAY TO THIS WELL-CONCEALED COUNTRY HOTEL is by the main Palma-Inca road. Alternatively, you can leave the main road about 8 km out of Palma and take the more varied country route via Santa Maria, Consell and Binissalem. On the way, a visit to the leather town of Inca makes a delightful detour for lovers of fine leather goods. From Inca, the country road leads directly to Costitx; nearby, San Porró is situated in a valley of almond trees and vegetable fields.

The rooms are furnished with pleasant, pale pine furniture. Suites have beautiful rustic fireplaces and dreamy views of the surrounding countryside or on to the hotel's patio. The owner, Maria Pilar Sánchez, is a talented communicator and catalyst who knows just how to mingle her guests so that they quickly feel at home. You might find three or four of them gathered to help Maria Pilar cook dinner in her typical Mallorcan country kitchen. Wine is very much a part of this *cuisine,* and in her kitchen bottles are on the go even as food is being prepared.

Nearby Costitx (3 km); beach of Ca'n Picafort (20 km)
Location on the edge of Costitx, signposted on the country road; own grounds and private car parking
Food breakfast, lunch, dinner
Price €€€-€€€€, including breakfast, food €€
Rooms 9; 3 doubles, 6 suites, all with bath, central heating, sound system, satellite TV, minibar
Facilities *salon*, outdoor swimming pool
Credit cards MC, V
Children welcome
Disabled no special facilities
Pets accepted
Closed never
Proprietor Maria Pilar Sánchez

MALLORCA

DEIÁ

LA RESIDENCIA
Elegant country hotel

Son Canals s/n, 07179 Deià
Tel 971 63 90 11 **Fax** 971 69 93 70
E-MAIL laresidencia@hotel-residencia.com **WEBSITE** www.hotel-laresidencia.com

ALMOST EVERYTHING ABOUT the Residencia (owned by Richard Branson) is out of the ordinary. Set above the road at the north end of the fashionable village of Deià, it is a cluster of creeper-covered stone buildings in beautiful tiered gardens. The core of the hotel is a 16thC manor house; the original olive mill is now the restaurant. There is also an annexe above the swimming pool behind the main building.

The interior of the hotel is exquisitely furnished with antique pieces, colourful rugs and fascinating modern art. Bedrooms vary in size, from smallish singles to an enormous suite in a separate building. All have lovely wooden furniture and many have antique or four-poster beds. There are bars and breakfast rooms in both parts of the hotel, though most people eat out on the terraces overlooking either the swimming pool (surrounded by elegant cypresses) or on the front lawns.

Another highlight is the hotel's acclaimed restaurant, El Olivo. Its loft ceiling, dripping candelabra, cane furniture and elegant tables, set among relics of the olive mill, make a wonderfully romantic setting for an excellent four- or eight-course dinner.

NEARBY Valldemosa (15 km); bay of Deià (3 km).
LOCATION at the exit of the village in the direction of Sóller; garden; parking
FOOD breakfast, lunch, dinner
PRICE €€€€, including breakfast, food €€-€€€
ROOMS 60; 38 doubles, 8 singles, 14 suites (3 with their own pool), all with bath, central heating, air conditioning, telephone, hairdryer
FACILITIES 2 restaurants, 4 *salons*, 4 bars, 2 open-air swimming pools, 1 indoor swimming pool, 2 tennis courts, cave, beauty salon, gym, sauna, health spa
CREDIT CARDS AE, MC, V **CHILDREN** under 10s welcome
DISABLED no special facilities **PETS** not accepted
CLOSED 1 Jul-15 Aug, 20-31 Oct, Christmas
PROPRIETOR John Rogers

Mallorca

Deià

Sa Perdrissa
~ COUNTRY HOTEL ~

Carretera Valldemosa-Deià, 07179 Deià
Tel 971 63 91 11 **Fax** 971 63 94 56

THIS FORMER MANOR HOUSE, situated on a hill, offers a bewitching view over the wild, craggy western coast of Mallorca. Opposite lies Deià, still described as an artists' town today, even though the *bon vivants* and artists have had to retreat to the island's interior because of spiralling housing costs. But peace still returns each evening to this much-frequented tourist town, with its picturesque alleys, and the magical church of John the Baptist, in whose churchyard novelist Robert Graves is buried. If you visit, be sure to make your way down to Cala Deià, its romantic little bay.

The history of the Pedrissa, once the property of Archbishop Ludwig Salvator of Austria, stretches back to the early 16th century. It has been lovingly restored with an eye to detail. Rooms have comfortable four-poster beds with turned mahogany posts, *trousseau* chests, stately cupboards with antique metal fittings – in other words, all the trappings of bourgeois wealth. Bathrooms have charming handmade tiles and some are painted with floral friezes.

The ancient olive press has been converted into a restaurant; menus major on regional specialities made with home-grown produce. An ample breakfast is served under shady pine trees.

~

Nearby Valldemosa (15 km); Sóller (15 km)
Location 2 km before the entrance to the village on the left-hand side, signposted
Food breakfast, lunch, dinner
Price €€€, including breakfast, food €€
Rooms 9; 5 doubles, 1 single, 3 suites, all with bath, central heating, air conditioning, telephone, hairdryer, satellite TV, minibar
Credit cards MC, V **Children** welcome only in July
Disabled no special facilities
Pets not accepted
Closed 15 Nov-1 Feb
Proprietor Sebastian Artigues

Mallorca

Deià

Es Moli
~ COUNTRY HOTEL BY THE SEA ~

Carretera Valldemosa-Deià s/n, 07179 Deià
Tel 971 63 90 00 **Fax** 971 63 93 33
E-mail esmoli@fehm.es **Website** www.ila.chateau.com/es-moli/

Deià's many visitors immediately appreciate its distinctive charm. For locals, the reality is not quite so palatable: once it was the haunt of Bohemians and artists, or anyone who cared to live in such a delightful place on a shoestring; now building plots, houses and apartments are barely affordable. Well, you don't have to worry about that if you stay at Es Moli, although you will pay a price that's in keeping. Although the hotel has 87 rooms, they are spread out in three separate buildings, so the feel is of a smaller place. The hotel's principal charm is its dramatic position in a ravine at the foot of a magical, steeply rising mountain. The view over the bay and beyond to the open sea is stupendous.

Bedrooms are generously proportioned. Period furniture, distinctive fabrics and flower pictures work together for a beguiling mood. Bathrooms are roomy, too, and tastefully tiled. Service is friendly and attentive. The huge terraces are elegantly furnished with English Lloyd Loom caneware. Beautiful table linen sets off the food. You'll find it hard to exhaust the many quiet corners for relaxation in the enchanting, 15,000 square-metre garden.

Nearby Valldemosa (15 km); Cala Deià beach. (4 km)
Location at the entrance to the village; large grounds and private car parking
Food breakfast, dinner
Price €€€€, including breakfast, food €€
Rooms 87; 9 singles, 75 doubles, 1 suite, 2 junior suites, all with bath, central heating, air conditioning, telephone, hairdryer, satellite TV (on request), minibar
Facilities restaurant, outdoor swimming pool, private beach, tennis court, hairdresser
Credit cards AE, MC, V **Children** welcome
Disabled no special facilities **Pets** not accepted
Closed 25 Oct-24 Apr
Manager Angel Fernandez

MALLORCA

ES PIL-LARI-SANFRANCISCO

POSADA D'ES MOLI
~ COUNTRY HOTEL ~

Camino Son Fangos, Es Pil-lari
TEL 971 26 05 93 **FAX** 971 26 93 68

FOR MANY GUESTS, Posada d'es Moli is unbeatable because it offers the peace of the countryside while being only a couple of kilometres from Mallorca's lively capital.

The manor house, wreathed in bougainvillea, was built in 1897. Rooms are furnished with exquisite antiques and boast generously proportioned bathrooms. To keep you active there is an indoor pool with hydro-massage; an outdoor pool; an immaculate putting green and practice net; AstroTurf tennis court; and bicycles.

The first-rate restaurant has a choice of international and Mallorcan cuisine. And it all comes at a price you'd expect from one of the island's best hotels.

Perhaps the most eye-catching feature of the estate, which comprises several buildings, is the restored windmill, one of many in the area once used to irrigate the fields.

~

NEARBY Palma (15 km).
LOCATION in countryside
FOOD breakfast, lunch, dinner
PRICE €€€-€€€€, including breakfast, food €€
ROOMS 17; 3 singles, 8 doubles, 4 junior suites, 2 suites, all with bath, central heating, air conditioning, telephone, hairdryer, satellite TV, minibar
FACILITIES restaurant, sitting room, bar, outdoor swimming pool, indoor swimming pool, tennis court, bicycles, putting green
CREDIT CARDS AE, MC, V
CHILDREN welcome
DISABLED no special facilities
PETS small dogs allowed
CLOSED Nov to Jan
PROPRIETOR Joan Rubi

MALLORCA

ESPORLES

S'HOSTAL D'ESPORLES
~ VILLAGE INN ~

Plaça d'Espanya 8, 07190 Esporles
Tel 971 61 02 02 **Fax** 971 61 02 02

ESPORLES IS ONE OF MALLORCA'S MANY typical villages, consisting basically of a main street on which everyday life is played out. S'Hostal d'Esporles, centrally situated in a row of terraced houses opposite the church, gives you a ringside seat. Plane trees make it pleasantly shady in hot weather; in fact the leafy surroundings are more like a garden than a village. The *hostal's* rooms are unpretentious, simply furnished but with love, in the local rustic style. It's a well-known local favourite, that has been in business for more than 70 years. Good Mallorcan cooking is available on request.

There are plenty of interesting trips to be made in the area, including La Granja estate, which dates back to the time of the Moors, and which today houses a worthwhile museum. There are also plenty of local craftwork centres, and places where you can discover how pastries and other Mallorcan specialities are made.

~

NEARBY La Granja museum (1.5 km).
LOCATION village square
FOOD breakfast, dinner on request
PRICE €€ including breakfast, food €-€€
ROOMS 11 doubles, all with shower/bath, central heating, hairdryer
FACILITIES restaurant, *salon*, TV room
CREDIT CARDS MC, V
CHILDREN welcome
DISABLED no special facilities
PETS not accepted
CLOSED never
PROPRIETOR Jaume Salas

Mallorca

Esporles

La Posada del Marques
~ Country hotel ~

Finca Es Verger, 07190 Esporles
Tel 971 61 12 30 **Fax** 971 61 12 13
Website www.posadamarques.com

This hotel has a sensational position in Es Verger mountains: it seems like an eagle's nest overlooking the village of Esporles, and is reached, predictably, by a tortuous road. The valley below is a beautiful and typical Mallorcan landscape, with tracts of pine woods and paths winding through wild thyme and rosemary bushes.

The 16thC estate has retained its original appearance, even after extensive renovation: the integrity of the interor remains intact, making you feel as if the place was always like this; yet up-to-date equipment and comforts are everywhere. There are staggering views down to the Bay of Parma.

The rooms and spacious suites exude good taste. Decoration is quite conservative, with period furniture, luxurious silk curtains in unobtrusive colours (such as light pink and yellow stripes); Art Nouveau style lamps give a charming, warm illumination. The bathrooms are luxuriously appointed. The restaurant pampers its guests either in the *tafona*, a restored oil mill, or on the terrace, with its breathtaking views. The light Mediterranean cuisine is the work of José Castoñer, who began his career at El Olivo in Deiá (see page 46). The wine list is particularly impressive.

~

Nearby Esporles (4 km); La Granja estate and national museum (8 km)
Location above village of Es Verger; own grounds and private car parking
Food breakfast, lunch, dinner
Price €€€€, including breakfast, food €€-€€€
Rooms 17; 12 doubles, 5 suites, all with bath, central heating, air conditioning, telephone, hairdryer, satellite TV, minibar
Facilities restaurant, sitting rooms, outdoor swimming pool
Credit cards AE, MC, V
Children welcome **Disabled** no special facilities
Pets small dogs allowed
Closed never
Proprietor Dietrich Weissenborn

MALLORCA

ESTELLENCS

SA PLANA PETIT HOTEL
~ SEASIDE HOTEL ~

Carrer Eusebi Pascal s/n, 07192 Estellencs
Tel 971 61 86 66 **Fax** 971 61 85 86

As its name suggests, this is a modest, small hotel, but it has much charm and offers everything you could expect at the price, which is fair, to say nothing of its superb setting. Every room has its own fireplace. Some of the beds are four-posters, with homely linen bedspreads. Local period furniture is generally of oak or stained pine. The dreamy terrace is a high spot, and so is the Mallorcan food, offered on the daily-changing menu. You will probably be offered the local cabbage soup served with unsalted bread; home-made sausages; or fish simply grilled on an an open fire in the garden. Vegetables are grown in the hotel's garden. There's an interesting local wine list.

Estellencs claims to offer views of the most beautiful sunsets on Mallorca, and its winding hillside streets make for picturesque strolls. The impressive church tower was once a watchtower that protected the village from pirates. There are a couple of charming restaurants that compare very well with those in Andratx or Banyulbufar.

Nearby Banyulbufar (7 km).
Location in village, own grounds and car parking
Food breakfast, dinner on request
Price €€, including breakfast, food €€
Rooms 5; 4 doubles, 1 room for 4 people, all with bath
Facilities recreation room, dining room
Credit cards DC, MC, V, Diners
Children welcome
Disabled no special facilities
Pets not accepted
Closed 10 Dec-15 Jan
Proprietor Paquita Bauza

MALLORCA

FELANITX

SA POSADA D'AUMALLIA
~ COUNTRY HOTEL ~

Camino Son Prohens 1027, 07200 Felanitx
TEL 971 58 26 57 **FAX** 971 58 32 69

FELANITX RESEMBLES A LARGE TOWN IN MINIATURE: it boasts a superb church with an imposing outside staircase; a lively market hall; a weekly market that happens every Sunday on the *Rambla;* and many corner shops that sell all manner of things, both practical and useless.

Just 4 km from Felanitx is the lovely Posada d'Aumallia, a perfect example of a classic manor house of the 1900s, decorated with contemporary rural elegance. As you enter the magnificent doorway and step into the main drawing room, you feel as if you've stepped back a hundred years. A fire crackles in the marble fireplace; an opulent, gold-framed mirror hangs above. To the right, an elegant grand piano and cello apparently wait to be played. The bedrooms are in local Mallorcan style, with antique furniture and locally woven fabrics. Bathrooms are a fair size. The half-panelled dining room exudes early 19thC charm.

Meanwhile, in the garden, peacocks shred the air with their strange cries, and the Mallorcan evening meal is announced. The mood could hardly be better. And the sea is just 7 km away from this idyll.

~

NEARBY Felanitx (4 km); Porto Colom beach (7 km).
LOCATION in the countryside; garden; parking
FOOD breakfast, dinner
PRICE €€-€€€, including breakfast, food €-€€
ROOMS 14 doubles, all with bath, central heating, air conditioning, telephone, hairdryer, satellite TV, minibar, safe
FACILITIES restaurant, sitting room, bar, outdoor swimming pool, tennis court, bicycles
CREDIT CARDS AE, MC, V
CHILDREN welcome
DISABLED no special facilities **PETS** not accepted
CLOSED never
MANAGER Maria Antonia Marti

MALLORCA

FORNALUTX

CA'N VERDERA
~ COUNTRY HOTEL ~

Carrer de Toros 1, 07109 Fornalutx
Tel 971 63 82 03 **Fax** 971 63 81 09
E-MAIL *canverdera@ctv.es* **WEBSITE** *www.canverdera.com*

C'AN VERDERA IS A GEM OF THE MID-1800S, carefully restored in keeping with the original architecture – arches, oriels and wooden balconies – and now furnished with choice designer furniture. The whitewashed walls help show off the cast-iron beds, the bright chairs upholstered with leather, and of course the curtains; and they are a helpful setting for the hotel's collection of contemporary art, much of it the work of local painters, that fill the walls. The location is in one of the most beautiful valleys on the island, the 'valley of the orange trees'.

If you stay here, take the opportunity to visit Fornalutx's town hall, where trophies, won in competitions for the nation's most beautiful village, fill the shelves. The place has been virtually built into a cliff; stones collected from the fields have been neatly laid into streets and footpaths. Green shutters decorate pretty façades and there are tubs of flowers in front of the doors: the definitive picture-postcard village.

NEARBY Sóller (3 km); beach (8 km).
LOCATION above the village, own grounds and private car parking
FOOD breakfast
PRICE €€€€, including breakfast
ROOMS 11; 9 doubles, 1 suite, 1 junior suite, all with bath, central heating, air conditioning, telephone, hairdryer, satellite TV
FACILITIES restaurants, sitting rooms, banqueting room, outdoor swimming pool, tennis court (on request, 5 minutes' walk)
CREDIT CARDS AE, MC, V
CHILDREN by arrangement
DISABLED no special facilities
PETS not accepted
CLOSED Dec-Jan
MANAGER Anna Celma

MALLORCA

LLOSETA

CA'S COMTE
~ COUNTRY HOTEL ~

Carrer Comte d'Aiamans 11, 07360 Lloseta
Tel 971 87 30 77 **Fax** 971 51 91 92
website *www.cascomte.com*

LLOSETA WAS ALWAYS A CHARMING TOWN, well aware of its traditions and identity, with active footwear, glass and ceramics industries. With the opening of the handsome Ca's Comte, it has now diversified confidently into the tourist industry.

The conversion of 18thC buildings formerly belonging to the Ayamans Palace has been done with flair. The bright patio functions as entrance hall and meeting point for guests and friends. From here stairs lead up to just four double rooms and four suites. They are airy, individually furnished, with lovely antique beds, rocking chairs, imposing armchairs and comfortable sofas weaving a pleasant atmosphere. In the modern bathrooms, chrome washbasins are set in clear glass, contrasting stylishly with the walls of rough-hewn stone. The lavish breakfast buffet will set you up for the day.

Nearby Bini (4 km).
Location in the village square; own grounds with private car parking
Food breakfas; lunch and dinner both on request
Price €€€, including buffet breakfast, food €€
Rooms 8; 4 doubles, 4 suites, all with bath, central heating, air conditioning, telephone, hairdryer, satellite TV
Facilities dining room, sitting rooms
Credit cards MC, V
Children welcome
Disabled no special facilities
Pets not accepted
Closed never
Proprietors Ramón Buñola family

Mallorca

Lluc Alcari

Costa d'Or
~ Country hotel by the sea ~

07179 Deià
Tel 971 63 90 25 **Fax** 971 63 93 47
E-mail costador@arrakis.es **Website** www.arrakis.es/costador/home.html

Mallorca's south-western coast is extremely beautiful: from Andratx to the little harbour town of Sóller, the dreamy coast road winds past the mountain villages of Estellencs, Banyulbufar, Valldemosa, Deià and Lluc Alcari, where a narrow road (but wide enough for cars) snakes its way down through a pine wood to this magical hotel. The view from its terrace and magnificent swimming pool is heart-stopping. The 37 bedrooms are fitted out with imposing mahogany furniture; characteristic Mallorcan blue-and-white fabric decorates windows and beds. The atmosphere is of peace and repose.

The hotel food is perfectly good, local cuisine, but gourmets in search of a change will find many excellent restaurants in the vicinity, either in the former artist's colony of Deià, or heading towards Sóller. See our restaurant section, pages 106-125.

~

Nearby Deià (2 km); Sóller (8 km).
Location on the hillside above Lluch Alcari, in own grounds with private car parking
Food breakfast, lunch, dinner
Price €€-€€€€, including breakfast, food €€
Rooms 37; 3 singles, 34 doubles, all with bath, central heating, telephone
Facilities restaurant, sitting rooms, outdoor swimming pool, tennis court
Credit cards MC, V
Children welcome
Disabled no special facilities
Pets not accepted
Closed 29 Oct-31 Mar
Proprietors Magraner family

MALLORCA

MANACOR

LA RESERVA ROTANA
~ COUNTRY HOTEL ~

Cami de s'Avall, 3 km, 07500 Manacor
Tel 971 84 56 85 **Fax** 971 55 52 58
E-mail hotel.rotana@jet.es **website** www.todoesp.es/la.rotana

A NARROW ASPHALT ROAD branches off the main road into Manacor, taking you through barren, unprepossessing countryside for about 3 km – after which the sight of this 17thC manor house comes as a pleasant surprise. Your first impression – from a cursory glance at the pool, bordered by manicured lawns is of a cultivated hotel, and once inside this is reinforced by the large sitting room with its impressive fireplace. The charm here is straight from the film *Out of Africa* – no coincidence, since the owner, Juan Theler, is a passionate big game hunter who has finally found a place to display his trophies. The grand but unpretentious atmosphere is no doubt down to the Princess Loretta zu Sayn Wittgenstein Hohenstein, Theler's wife, who masterminded the choice of fabrics, furnishings and ornaments and pictures. Aristocratic country-house style lends an undeniable glamour.

Stressed-out guests comes here for relaxation; and quite possibly find it on the hotel's nine-hole golf course; or in the sophisticated Mediterranean *cuisine*.

~

Nearby Porto Cristo (20 km).
Location 3 km from the main Manacor road (signposted); own grounds and private car parking
Food breakfast, lunch, dinner
Price €€€€, including breakfast, food €€-€€€
Rooms 21; 1 single, 10 doubles, 1 suite, 9 junior suites, all with bath, central heating, air conditioning, telephone, hairdryer, satellite TV, minibar
Facilities restaurant, banqueting room for 20 people, sitting room, outdoor swimming pool, tennis court, gym, sauna, 9-hole golf course
Credit cards AE, MC, V **Children** welcome **Disabled** no special facilities
Pets not accepted
Closed no fixed times
Proprietor Juan Ramón Theler

Mallorca

Manacor

Son Amoixa Vell
~ *Finca* hotel ~

Carretera Cales de Mallorca-Manacor, km 3.4, 07500 Manacor
Tel 971 18 39 73 **Fax** 670 88 15 34

Amoixa Vell stands in 20 hectares of romantic, undulating countryside dotted with lemon, fig and almond trees. Its history goes back to the 16th century; the main building's present imposing appearance has evolved over hundreds of years. The suites, bedrooms and bathrooms are generously proportioned and tastefully decorated. Rough-plastered, white-washed walls give the restaurant a rustic feel, emphasized by the beautiful stone arches. A Mallorcan and a German cook are on hand, and the food competes with the best on the island. There's a wide range of activites to fill your time; but just mellowing out for an evening in the cosy sitting room with a glass of wine is something special. This is for you if you prize individuality and high standards. More than one guest has described it as 'paradise'.

~

Nearby Manacor (6 km); beautiful bathing beach of Cala Romantica (5 km)
Location between Manacor and Cales de Mallorca; own grounds and private parking
Food breakfast, dinner
Price €€€€, including breakfast, food €€
Rooms 15; 10 doubles, 2 junior suites, 2 suites, 1 apartment, all with bath, central heating, air conditioning, telephone, hairdryer, satellite TV, sound system, minibar
Facilities restaurant, sitting rooms, outdoor swimming pool, tennis court, gym, sauna
Credit cards MC, V
Children welcome
Disabled no special facilities
Pets not accepted
Closed 1 Nov-25 Dec
Manager Hans Jörg Geisen

MALLORCA

MANACOR

SON GENER
FINCA HOTEL

Carretera Son Servera, km 3, 07550 Son Servera
TEL 971 18 36 12 **FAX** 971 18 35 91
E-MAIL songener@todoesp.es

SON GENER IS A few kilometres beyond Manacor in the direction of Artá, in pleasant countryside. The owner is a creative architect and designer – and this will come as no surprise to those with an eye for details such as artful exposure of architectural structure, and a modern, minimalist interior that accentuates furniture, tasteful fabrics and decorative objects. Sitting rooms, bedrooms and terraces are alive with Mediterranean light: very few other places to stay on Mallorca are as well designed in this respect. It's an ambience that corresponds exactly to many Northern Europeans' idea of what Mediterranean lifestyle is about.

This is the place to stay if you like artificial pearls: just 4 km away is Manacor, Mallorca's second town and the Mecca of the artificial pearl, with dozens of shops selling what claim to be the best quality and most brilliant of their kind.

NEARBY Manacor (4 km); Artá monastery (10 km).
LOCATION at the edge of Manacor heading towards Artá, signposted
FOOD breakfast, dinner
PRICE €€€€, including breakfast, food €€–€€€
ROOMS 10 suites, all with bath, central heating, air conditioning, telephone, satellite TV, minibar
FACILITIES restaurant, wine cellar, swimming pool, bicycles
CREDIT CARDS AE, MC, V
CHILDREN welcome
DISABLED no special facilities
PETS not accepted
CLOSED never
PROPRIETOR Antonio Estevaa Cañellas

MALLORCA

MONTUIRI

ES FIGUERAL NOU
~ COUNTRY HOTEL ~

Carretera Montuiri-San Joan, km 0.7, 07230 Montuiri
TEL 971 64 67 64 **FAX** 971 64 67 47

THE LITTLE VILLAGE OF MONTUIRI, perched on its hill, is visible from quite a distance. When you arrive, you find all the houses charmingly huddled around the centre. From here, take the road leading out of the village, past terraces of yellow houses, to Es Figueral Nou.

The 15thC estate has been completely renovated. A flight of steps leads to the hotel's attractive vestibule, which doubles as a resting place. The hall opens on to a large terrace, with a wonderful view on to the plain below, typical of the scenery of Mallorca's centre.

Fine antique furniture, some of it family pieces, sets the style in the generously proportioned rooms. Two swimming pools, a tennis court, a gym, sauna and whirlpool will keep you busy and/or relaxed. The spacious, airy restaurant serves Mallorcan delicacies.

~

NEARBY Montuiri (1 km); Es Trenc beach (30 km).
LOCATION at the exit to the village; in own grounds with private car parking
FOOD breakfast, lunch, dinner
PRICE €€€€, including breakfast, food €€
ROOMS 18; 17 doubles, 1 junior suite, all with bath, central heating, air conditioning, telephone, hairdryer, satellite TV, minibar
FACILITIES restaurant, sitting rooms, 2 heated pools (1 covered), tennis court, gym, sauna, whirlpool, children's playground
CREDIT CARDS AE, MC, V
CHILDREN welcome
DISABLED no special facilities
PETS not accepted
CLOSED never
PROPRIETOR Vicente Grande

MALLORCA

MOSCARI

CA'N CALCO
~ VILLAGE INN ~

Carrer Campanet 1, 07313 Selva-Moscari
Tel 971 51 52 60 **Fax** 971 52 60

Time still passes slowly in the little village of Moscari: mass tourism is still at a distance, and the villagers enjoy their peace and quiet. They sit, as their grandparents did, in front of their houses, or at a street café with a *Hierbas,* or sit in the bar playing dice and cards.

This little *finca* hotel, with just five junior suites, is one of a few truly successful examples of pure modern interior design in Mallorca. Dominant colours are restricted to white, sand and black. The walls are whitewashed, and this is combined with the natural sandstone to give a pleasing, warm feel, especially in the restaurant and breakfast room. Delicate black cast-iron furniture, upholstered in natural white completes the effect. Everything is minimalist and tasteful. The kitchen specializes in fresh fish dishes, including the famous *caldereta,* a fine shellfish stew.

The owners have a mission to make Mallorcan art known to their guests and mount regular exhibitions of both painting and sculpture.

~

Nearby Pollença (25 km).
Location at the exit to the village; in own grounds, private car parking
Food breakfast, dinner
Price €€€, including breakfast, food €€
Rooms 5 junior suites, all with bath and hydromassage, central heating, air conditioning, telephone, hairdryer, satellite TV, minibar
Facilities restaurant, sitting room, outdoor swimming pool
Credit cards MC, V
Children welcome
Disabled 1 room with large bath, easy access for wheelchairs
Pets small dogs accepted
Closed Nov
Proprietor Jaime Vives Mir

Mallorca

Orient

L'Hermitage
~ Country hotel ~

Carretera Alaró-Bunyola, 07349 Orient
Tel 971 18 03 03 **Fax** 971 18 04 11

The great attraction of L'Hermitage is its setting, tucked away in a beautiful fruit-growing valley in the mountains, miles from the beaten track (no mean achievement in Mallorca these days). It consists of a somewhat strange selection of buildings: a narrow 17thC stone manor house (with tower), a two-storey modern block overlooking an orchard and a totally separate cloister with 16 twisted stone pillars enclosing lemon and orange trees. Only four of the bedrooms are in the old house. These have tiny windows peerinbg out of thick walls, making the rooms beautifully cool but also very dim; with polished furntiure on old tiled floors, they have much more character than the modern rooms - though these are also cool and comfortable, with palatial bathrooms.

There is a warren of tiny public rooms in the old part of te hotel, including an elegant downstairs sitting room and a cosy upstairs one with an open fire. In contrast, the dining room in the old olive mill is enormous. It still has a sloping, beamed ceiling and the original grinding stones, which make an admirable table for the generous buffet breakfast.

Nearby Buñola (10 km); Alaró (10 km).
Location in the Tramuntana mountains, 1 km from Orient; garden; parking
Food breakfast, lunch, dinne
Price €€€€, includingl. breakfast, à la carte meals €€-€€€
Rooms 24, all with bath, central heating, telephone, minibar, satellite TV, safe, hairdryer
Facilities restaurant, 2 sitting rooms, sitting room with fireplace, bar, terrace, sauna, 2 tennis courts, heated swimming pool
Credit cards AE, DC, MC, V **Children** over 12s welcome
Disabled no special facilities **Pets** small dogs allowed
Closed 10 Nov-30 Jan
Proprietor E. Tietz

MALLORCA

PALMA

HOTEL BORN
~ HISTORIC TOWN HOTEL ~

Carrer Sant Jaume 3, 07012 Palma
TEL 971 71 29 42 **FAX** 971 71 86 18

CARRER SANT JAUME, an important conduit between the Plaça Espana and the Plaça Joan Carles, is in Palma's *Casco antiguo* (old town), and on it is the Hotel Born. The district is designated a national treasure, part of the Monumento Nacional de España. One fine façade succeeds another; playful oriels jut out from the fronts of houses; behind wooden slatted windows hang heavy fabrics of brocade, velvet and silk. Over the centuries, pedestrians have polished the cobbles to a high gloss.

Inside the hotel, great marble pillars support the Gothic arches of the entrance hall. This opens on to the patio, lush with palm trees, where in summer they serve a Mallorcan breakfast with authentic local *ensaimada* (pastries). A stone staircase sweeps in a broad and elegant arc up to the first floor. Bedrooms are comfortable and charmingly furnished; suites are considerably more spacious.

Just around the corner from the hotel is the famous Avenida Jaime III, with its elegant shops.

~

NEARBY old town; beach (2 km).
LOCATION in town centre; own car parking
FOOD breakfast
PRICE €€-€€€€, including breakfast
ROOMS 35; 26 doubles, 6 singles, 3 suites, all with bath, central heating, air conditioning, telephone, satellite TV, minibar only in the suites
FACILITIES patio
CREDIT CARDS AE, MC, V
CHILDREN welcome
DISABLED no special facilities
PETS not accepted
CLOSED never
MANAGER Miguel Angel Frontera

Mallorca

Palma

Palaçio Casa Calesa
~ Historic Town Hotel ~

Carrer Miramar 8, 07001 Palma
Tel 971 71 54 00 **Fax** 971 72 15 79
E-MAIL reserves@fehm.es **WEBSITE** www.fehm.es

Palma's aristocratic palaces can be very grand indeed: their architecture puts mere commoners in their place. Casa Calesa is no exception, and has the added interest of being open to outsiders – many of the palaces are still family-owned and may not be visited.

Its architecture is a textbook example of 17thC style, and much of the furniture has the opulence to match. By contrast, some of the bedrooms are fitted out in what could be called American style, with white-lacquered rattan furniture upholstered in flowery fabrics – possibly an acquired taste. An English tea is served in the afternoon in the Monet kitchen.

Nearby you can visit the royal palace and the gothic cathedral (La Seu), whose spectacular position a stone's throw from the Mediterranean shore is unique in Europe. Don't miss the cathedral's stained glass windows, particularly striking at sunrise and sunset.

~

Nearby harbour (500 m); fish market and market hall (1.5 km)
Location in the centre; own parking
Food breakfast
Price €€€€, including breakfast
Rooms 11; 5 doubles, 2 suites with terrace, 1 presidential suite, 3 junior suites, all with bath, central heating, air conditioning, telephone, hairdryer, satellite TV, minibar, tea and coffee making facilities, safe
Facilities sitting rooms, covered swimming pool, gym, whirlpool, sauna, sun terrace
Credit cards AE, MC, V
Children welcome
Disabled no special facilities
Pets not accepted
Closed never
Manager Sonia Marzo

Mallorca

Palma

Palau Sa Font
~ Town hotel ~

Carrer Apuntadores 38, 07012 Palma
Tel 971 71 22 77 **Fax** 971 71 26 18
E-mail info@palausafont.com **website** www.palausafont.com

At the peaceful end of the Carrer Apuntadores (with its many restaurants and bars to draw the tourists) stands the Palau Sa Font, a former 16thC bishop's palace now dressed up in modern designer garb. In case you are in any doubt, this will hit you between the eyes as you penetrate the entrance hall, where brilliant red leather chairs make a striking contrast with the subtle colour of ochre sandstone walls.

The hotel's 19 bedrooms reveal a purist's taste in furnishings. Beds are a generous size. Wrought-iron bedside tables carry lamps with chrome feet and frosted glass shades, giving out a warm light. Chairs are covered in brightly coloured leather – orange, red or dark blue. Bathrooms are in a cool, high-tech style with much use of mirrors.

This is a breakfast-only hotel, but there are plenty of other eating places in the neighbourhood (as well as on Carrer Apuntadores) and just around the corner, in the lively Plaça Drassana, every other bar offers delicious *tapas*.

~

Nearby Es Molinar beach (3 km).
Location old town; garage parking nearby
Food breakfast
Price €€-€€€€, including breakfast
Rooms 19; 4 singles, 14 doubles of varying size, 1 junior suite with terrace, all with bath, central heating, air conditioning, telephone, hairdryer, satellite TV, minibar, safe
Facilities sitting room, bar, plunge pool, Jacuzzi
Credit cards AE, MC, V
Children welcome
Disabled no special facilities
Pets by agreement
Closed never
Proprietors Tom Gössmann and Ricarda Söhnlein

Mallorca

Palma

Hotel Portixol
~ Town hotel by the harbour ~

Carrer Sirena 27, 07006 Palma
Tel 971 27 18 00 **Fax** 971 27 50 25
website www.portixol.com

The Hotel Portixol, right on Palma's promenade, was saved from ruin in 1988 by Swede Mikael Lundström. The restoration of the building and its purist furnishings can claim to be a benchmark for contemporary interior design: several innovative Mallorcan hotels have followed Lundström's ideas. The rooms and stairwell are carpeted in sisal. Designer lamps cast exactly the right light over beds and tables. The TV is concealed in its own cupboard. Bathrooms are on the small side, but very practically fitted out. More than half the rooms have a balcony with an incomparable view over Palma, the harbour and promenade, and the Paseo Maritimo. Depending on the cook's mood that day, the hotel restaurant is either good or average, and many a meal seems unjustly expensive: we hope that the management will note this commonly expressed opinion of the hotel. The Portixol's bar is a popular meeting place for local residents.

Above the hotel stands the imposing, circular fortress of Castillo de Bellver, a splendid backdrop; and to provide smaller-scale, more human interest, the harbour of Portixol is close by. It is full of unpretentious little boats owned by Mallorcans: seeing them set off at weekends for fishing or sunbathing trips is a pleasant diversion.

Nearby central Palma (3 km).
Location on the outskirts of the city; parking in front of the hotel
Food breakfast, lunch, dinner
Price €€€-€€€€, including breakfast, food €€-€€€
Rooms 24; 6 singles, 16 doubles, 1 suite, 1 penthouse, all with bath, central heating, air conditioning, telephone, hairdryer, satellite TV, minibar
Facilities restaurant, sitting room, bar, outdoor swimming pool
Credit cards AE, MC, V **Children** welcome
Disabled no special facilities **Pets** not accepted
Closed never
Proprietor Mikael Lundström

Mallorca

Palma

San Lorenzo
~ Town hotel ~

Carrer San Llorenc 14, 07012 Palma
Tel 971 72 82 00 **Fax** 971 71 19 01
E-mail sanlorenzo@fehm.es **Website** www.fehm.es/pmi/sanlorenzo

The narrow Carrer San Llorenc, with its hotel of the same name, lies in the heart of Palma's old town, only a few metres from the harbour area with its picturesque streets and the Plaça Drassana, where in times gone by, ship's ropes were manufactured, hence the name. The area comes alive at night – it's a meeting place both for locals and newcomers from all over Europe.

A glimpse through the wrought-iron gate reveals the San Lorenzo's welcoming character. At the end of the 1980s, it was one of the first Mallorcan hotels to have new life breathed into its ancient walls by modern style. When it opened, it caused quite a stir: the owners' courage in opening such a hotel in the heart of Palma was much admired – conventional wisdom had it that most visitors to Mallorca prefer the beach and the sea. The (few) rooms are decorated in Provençal style. Beautiful design features, paintings by native artists and *objets d'art* reveal the originality of the owners' taste. The two rooms on the street can be rather noisy at night, so be sure to ask for a room at the back.

~

Nearby harbour (500 m).
Location in the old town
Food breakfast
Price €€€€, including breakfast
Rooms 6; 4 doubles, 2 junior suites, all with bath, central heating, air conditioning, telephone, hairdryer, satellite TV, minibar
Facilities bar, sitting room, outdoor swimming pool
Credit cards AE, MC, V
Children welcome
Disabled no special facilities
Pets by arrangement
Closed never
Manager Rudolf Schmid

MALLORCA

PALMA-EL TERRENO

HOSTAL CORONA
~ SUBURBAN HOTEL ~

Carrer Santa Rita 17, 07014 Palma
Tel 971 73 19 35 **Fax** 971 73 19 35
E-MAIL hostalcorona@hotmail.com

In the 1950s, the area of El Terreno, beneath the mighty stronghold of Castillo de Bellver, was one of Palma's classiest. Celebrities such as Marlene Dietrich, Frank Sinatra and Liza Minelli enjoyed huge success in the district's Titos nightclub. Times have changed since then: these days, El Terreno is a lacklustre suburb, and the Hostal Corona can claim to be its principal beacon of light. It has a unique charm that makes it the perfect address for those on a budget who want to make the most of life, and who appreciate a certain Bohemian ambience.

Rooms are simply furnished. Some have old wooden beds and pretty curtains; all have beautiful floor tiles dating from around 1900. Native Mallorcans and guests mingle in the enchanting garden with its bar, and in the first-floor restaurant. The cooking is done by owner Margarita Navarra.

~

Nearby Palma's centre (4 km); Castillo de Bellver (about 30 minutes' walk uphill); beaches (Playa de Palma 12 km).
Location El Terreno district; garden; private car parking
Food breakfast, dinner
Price €€, including breakfast, food €-€€
Rooms 10 doubles, bathrooms not en suite
Facilities restaurant, 2 bars
Credit cards MC, V
Children welcome
Disabled no special facilities
Pets not accepted
Closed 1 Nov-15 Feb
Proprietors Margarita and Cristobal Navarra

Mallorca

Peguera

Hotel Bahia
~ Seaside Hotel ~

Avenida Peguera 81, 07160 Peguera
Tel 971 68 61 00 **Fax** 971 68 61 04

Peguera is a perennially popular holiday resort: in season, you get the feeling that most of the population are visitors from abroad, many making long stays; you don't see many Spanish words on noticeboards and signposts. Its quality as a resort has improved enormously over the last few years: the harbour promenade has been revamped and the main street, with its many shops, is now a pedestrian zone and good for wandering around of an evening.

The Bahia's name aptly refers to its location in a bay. We like its individual furnishings and the bedrooms' colour schemes, using delicate colours such as saffron, powder blue and sand. It's inviting and comfortable, neither cluttered with furniture, nor coldly minimalist. Terracotta-coloured bedspreads and pretty chairs in the same colour have a certain Mediterranean flair. There's an outdoor pool for summer, and a covered one for winter. The service is excellent: you'll feel well and truly looked after here.

Nearby Port d'Andratx (8 km), beach (100 m)
Location in the town; own garden and private car parking
Food breakfast
Price €€€, including breakfast
Rooms 52; 5 singles, 47 doubles, all with bath, central heating, air conditioning, telephone, hairdryer, satellite TV, safe
Facilities sitting room, bar, outdoor swimming pool, covered pool, sauna, putting green, darts, table tennis
Credit cards AE, MC, V
Children welcome
Disabled no special facilities
Pets not accepted
Closed 8 Nov-6 Apr
Manager Nuria Nadal

Mallorca

Pina

Son Xotano
~ Country hotel ~

Carrtera Pina-Sencelles km 1.5, 07630 Pina
Tel 971 87 25 00 **Fax** 971 87 25 01
E-mail sonxotano@mallorcanet.com **Website** www.mallorca.com/sonxotano

Son Xotano, dating from around 1700, is a former *possesio* or country seat converted to a comfortable modern hotel without compromising the original character of the house. All rooms are decorated in Mallorcan style, with good reproduction furniture that recreates the domestic lifestyle of the now almost vanished local landed gentry. The old kitchen is no longer in use; instead, the owner, a gourmet of the first order, has extended the old *celler mallorquin* (cellar), turning it into a restaurant offering regional dishes of the finest quality.

The estate has its own horses and carriages, which guests can use for expeditions and picnics. Or you can just mellow out beside the outdoor pool under the shade of brushwood.

The nearby village, Pina, is just a few kilometres from Porreres, but by contrast a delightfully sleepy backwater. You're well away from it all here.

Nearby Porreres (6 km)
Location signposted in Pina – 1.5 km from the village; own grounds and private car parking
Food breakfast, lunch, dinner
Price €€€, including breakfast, food €€
Rooms 16; 8 doubles, 8 suites, all with bath, central heating, air conditioning, telephone, hairdryer, satellite TV, minibar
Facilities restaurant (Es Menjador des Canonges), conference room, outdoor swimming pool, riding, carriage rides, bicycles, massages
Credit cards AE, MC, V
Children welcome
Disabled no special facilities
Pets not accepted
Closed never
Proprietor Pedro Ramonell

MALLORCA

POLLENÇA

CALA SANT VICENÇ
~ SEASIDE HOTEL ~

Carrer Maressers 2, 07469 Cala Sant Vicenç/Pollença
TEL 971 53 02 50 **FAX** 0971 53 20 84
E-MAIL cala@pobox.com
WEBSITE www.pobox.com/hotel.cala.sant.vicenç

EN ROUTE TO PUERTO POLLENÇA, few drivers notice the country road signposted to Cala Sant Vicenç. Follow it, and you will come upon a small, enchanted bay that has remained unspoiled by mass tourism. The road leads past a complex of holiday and weekend homes with lovely gardens, owned mainly by Mallorquins, to this fabulous spot.

There is no problem finding the hotel among the palm trees. It is painted a strong terracotta colour, and has an isolated position on a promontory. As soon as you arrive, you will notice the friendly, attentive mood radiated by the Suau family. You get views to the bay, with its surrounding cliffs, from the terraces, the rooms and the outdoor swimming pool; and it's a 300-m walk to the sea. Decoration is simple and traditional: mahogany furniture, heavy fabrics and vividly coloured bedspreads are smart and acceptable, if not very imaginative. British companies such as Hogg Robinson Travel have singled it out as a 'Best small hotel'. There are two restaurants, the Cavall Bernat (classic Mediterranean fare) and the Trattoria (Italian cuisine); in both, the food reaches a high standard.

~

NEARBY Pollença (7 km).
LOCATION off the Puerto Pollença road, on remote bay; own grounds and private car parking
FOOD breakfast, lunch, dinner
PRICE €€€-€€€€ including breakfast, food €€-€€€
ROOMS 38; 4 singles, 19 doubles, 15 suites, all with bath, central heating, air conditioning, telephone, hairdryer, satellite TV, minibar
FACILITIES 2 restaurants, sitting rooms, outdoor swimming pool, gym, sauna
CREDIT CARDS AE, MC, V
CHILDREN welcome
DISABLED no special facilities
PETS not accepted **CLOSED** Dec and Jan
PROPRIETORS Suau family

Mallorca

Pollença

Hotel Juma
~ Town hotel ~

Plaça Mayor 9, 07460 Pollença
Tel 971 53 50 02 **Fax** 971 53 41 55

The Hotel Juma is located on Pollença's lively square, occupying a prominent corner site. The reception area and the spacious restaurant, on an elevated ground floor, make a friendly meeting place for locals.

The bedrooms offer the sort of space and comfort you'd expect: adequate beds, built-in cupboards and furnishings typical of a modest Spanish town hotel, with an antique here and there. Bathrooms are clean, but somewhat small. Breakfast is served in the restaurant or on the terrace.

Pollença, with its population of 11,000, is one of the most beautiful small towns on Mallorca. There are many shops in the narrow streets that sell local wares, including textiles, leather goods, music and ceramics. The classical music festival, held in August and September in the monastery of Santo Domingo and attracting world-famous stars such as Montserrat Caballé and José Carreras, is well known in Mallorca and beyond.

It is worth making the climb up the Calvary hill (365 steps, one for every day of the year); you will be rewarded with great views over the Puig de Maria, opposite, and the Hermitage.

~

Nearby Puerto Pollença (6 km).
Location market square; private parking
Food breakfast
Price €€-€€€, including breakfast
Rooms 7; 2 singles, 5 doubles, all with bath (except 1 single), central heating, air conditioning, telephone, hairdryer, satellite TV, safe
Facilities sitting room, bar
Credit cards AE, MC, V
Children welcome
Disabled no special facilities **Pets** not accepted
Closed 15 Nov-15 Dec
Proprietor Antonio Cifre

Mallorca

Porreras

Sa Bassa Rotja
~ Country hotel ~

Camino Sa Pedrera `Finca Son Orell', 07260 Porreras
Tel 971 16 82 25 **Fax** 971 16 65 63

SA BASSA ROTJA IS ON A LOVINGLY RESTORED ESTATE surrounded by vineyards and vegetable plantations, just 3 km from the typically Mallorcan village of Porreras, in the heart of the island. Plants are gradually colonizing the barren agricultural land around the hotel.

All the rooms are individually furnished and very comfortable. A fine library and delightful sitting rooms make charming places in which to while away the hours, but the hotel's high spots are definitely the recreational and therapeutic facilities. There is a large outdoor pool and a heated covered pool, as well as bicycles. As for health and well-being, put yourself in the expert, caring hands of Angela Jung, who offers Ayurvedic treatments, aromatherapy and massage.

The excellent restaurant offers Mallorcan and international dishes.

Nearby Campos (10 km); Es Trenc beach nature reserve (18 km)
Location 3 km from the town centre
Food breakfast, lunch, dinner
Price €€-€€€€
Rooms 25; 10 doubles, 3 singles, 12 suites, all with bath, central heating, air conditioning, telephone, hairdryer, satellite TV, minibar, sound system
Facilities 2 tennis courts, heated indoor swimming pool, outdoor swimming pool, gym, therapy centre, sauna, Turkish bath, Jacuzzi, beauty salon, *boccia* playing field, archery, bicycles
Credit cards AE, MC, V
Children welcome
Disabled good access
Pets not accepted
Closed never
Manager Guillermo Rosselló

MALLORCA

PORTALS NOUS

HOTEL BENDINAT
~ SEASIDE HOTEL ~

Avenida Bendinat 58, 07015 Portals Nous
TEL 971 67 57 25 **FAX** 971 67 72 76

THIS CAN CLAIM TO BE one of Mallorca's most beautiful country hotels that also has a sea view. Just before reaching it, you pass through an upmarket area of luxury villas, where prosperous Mallorcans from Palma have their summer residences. This sets the scene for the hotel's exclusive feature – its spectacular position. Built in the 1950s, it has lost none of its original charm, even after comprehensive (but careful) restoration in 1993. Plants are gradually colonizing the barren agricultural land around the hotel.

Especially good views are to be had over the sea and bay of Palma Nova from the upper storey of the main building, in which some of the 46 rooms are to be found. The original Edwardian English furnishings have been retained in the rooms; they suit the house and create an elegant ambience. Magnificent pines cast the necessary shade on the terrace, where lunch and dinner are served from May to October. Tasteful cane furniture and immaculate table linen are what you'd expect, and what you get, together with attentive service. Many Mallorcan regulars come here at the weekend for the good food.

~

NEARBY Portals Nous; marina (2 km).
LOCATION 9 km SW of Palma; close to the sea, signposted Hotel Bendinat
FOOD breakfast, lunch, dinner
PRICE €€€€, including breakfast, food €€
ROOMS 46; 38 doubles, 2 singles, 6 junior suites, all with bath, central heating, air conditioning, telephone, hairdryer, satellite TV, minibar, safe
FACILITIES restaurant, sitting rooms, outdoor swimming pool
CREDIT CARDS AE, MC, V
CHILDREN welcome
DISABLED no special facilities
PETS not accepted **CLOSED** 1 Nov-1 Feb
MANAGER Bertram von Ondarza

MALLORCA

PORT D'ANDRATX

VILLA ITALIA
~ SEASIDE HOTEL ~

Camino de San Carlos 13, 07157 Port d'Andratx
TEL 971 67 40 11 **FAX** 971 67 33 50

PORT D'ANDRATX IS ONE OF MALLORCA'S most beautiful natural harbours. Many foreigners, Germans especially, have settled here in the last few years; in the process, the formerly pine-clad mountains have been completely built up and the little harbour has developed into a sophisticated tourist resort. The charm of the fishing village has been compromised through the introduction of – among other things – designer boutiques, expensive interior design shops and supposedly good restaurants; however, along the promenade at sunset you can still catch something of the place's original character.

The splendidly situated Villa Italia hotel remains a sought-after address for guests who are visiting the harbour in search of real estate. Everything about it is correspondingly grand. Many rooms have round bathtubs, Roman pillars, the finest bed linen and stuccoed ceilings. The restaurant is recommended. From its terrace you have a view of the harbour basin, with all the bustle of fishing vessels coming and going.

~

NEARBY San Telm, with beach and island nature reserve of Dragonera (8 km).
LOCATION above the harbour; garden and private car parking
FOOD breakfast, lunch, dinner
PRICE €€€€, including breakfast, food €€-€€€
ROOMS 16; 10 doubles, 6 suites, all with bath, air conditioning, telephone, minibar, satellite TV
FACILITIES restaurant, terraces, swimming pool, sauna
CREDIT CARDS AE, MC, V
CHILDREN welcome
DISABLED access difficult
PETS not accepted
CLOSED first 2 weeks Dec
MANAGER Antonio Martin

Mallorca

Puigpunyent

Son Net
~ Country hotel ~

Parcelacion Son Net, s/n, Castillo Son Net, 07194 Puigpunyent
Tel 971 14 70 00 **Fax** 971 14 70 01
E-mail son.net@jet.es **Website** www.sonnet.es

This can claim to be not only one of Mallorca's most stunning hotels, but all the Balearics'. It has a spectacular mountain setting, with sweeping views into the valley; it has the distinctive architecture and decoration of an authentic local 17thC manor house; and it also benefits from a lush garden and elegant (30-m) pool complex. American millionaire David Stein developed it as his dream hotel in the mid-1990s, and now others can dream here too, in total peace. The rooms and suites are decorated with modern flair. Large bathrooms are fitted out with magnificent free-standing baths and black African granite on the walls. The Sa Tafona restaurant, an old oil mill, is presided over by Xisco Martorell - see page 121. Six excellent golf courses are only half an hour away. The health and beauty centre in the cellar, without natural light, could benefit from being extended. On special evenings, Lucullan delicacies from around the world are served on the magnificent terraces.

~

Nearby Palma (20 km); mountain village of Galilea (7 km)
Location on a hill above the village; own grounds and private car parking
Food breakfast, lunch, dinner
Price €€€€, including breakfast, food €€€
Rooms 29; 25 doubles and suites, 4 king' suites, all with central heating, air conditioning, satellite TV, minibar, telephone, safe
Facilities 2 restaurants, 2 sitting rooms, bar, pool, sauna, beauty salon, massage, gym, tennis court
Credit cards AE, MC, V
Children welcome
Disabled lift **Pets** not accepted
Closed never
Proprietor David Stein

Mallorca

Randa

Es Recó de Randa
~ Country hotel ~

Carrer Font 13, 07629 Randa
Tel 971 66 09 97 **Fax** 971 66 25 58

Much of Es Recó's charm is in its splendid, open views, but the interior has its attractions, too, decorated in Mallorcan country-house style: local-style wooden furniture in light pine, Spanish fabrics and the occasional piece of antique furniture as an eye-catcher. The highly regarded restaurant (see page 122) is well known throughout the island for its home cooking, and its five-course sample menus can claim to be the best way for anyone to get to know Mallorca's culinary specialities. Beautiful walks can be taken from the hotel, such as the climb through a pine wood to the 15thC monastery complex of Santuari de Sant Honorat.

The nearby village of Randa sits between two mountains whose origins are the subject of a quaint local legend. One of the giants who lived on Mallorca wanted to build a house in the north. But the best building materials were to be found in the south. To cut a long story short, that's where he headed. Where Randa is today, he lost his footing, spilling the contents of the two baskets he was carrying, and this is how the mountains of Randa and Galdent appeared.

~

Nearby Playa de Palma beach (20 km)
Location at the edge of the village; in own grounds, with private car parking
Food breakfast, lunch, dinner
Price €€€-€€€€, including breakfast, food €€-€€€
Rooms 14 doubles, all with bath, central heating, air conditioning, telephone, satellite TV, minibar
Facilities restaurant, sitting rooms, outdoor swimming pool, sauna
Credit cards AE, MC, V
Children welcome
Disabled no special facilities
Pets not accepted
Closed never
Manager Manuel Salamanca

MALLORCA

RUBERTS

SON JORDÀ
FINCA HOTEL

Ruberts, 07410 Sencelles
TEL 971 58 51 23 **FAX** 971 81 32 62

THE VILLAGE OF RUBERTS CONSISTS OF THE CHURCH, a few houses scattered about and the *finca* hotel Son Jordà. The 15thC building looks relatively modest from the outside, but the interior is something else, having benefitted from a particularly successful renovation. New windows and beautiful bathrooms have been added, and a sitting room and dining room. The bedrooms are furnished in classic Spanish style: rustic double beds are of turned mahogany, and Mallorcan bedspreads give a cosy feel. In summer, the generously sized outdoor pool offers a refreshing dip; in the autumn and winter months, guests sit by the fire for a chat. Staff are attentive but unobtrusive; a place where you can relax and be yourself.

NEARBY Alcudia beach (25 km).
LOCATION near the church; garden and private car parking
FOOD breakfast, lunch, dinner
PRICE €€€, including breakfast, food €-€€
ROOMS 18 doubles, all with bath, central heating, air conditioning, telephone, hairdryer, satellite TV, minibar
FACILITIES restaurant, outdoor swimming pool, solarium, tennis court, bicycles
CREDIT CARDS not accepted
CHILDREN welcome
DISABLED no special facilities
PETS not accepted
CLOSED never
PROPRIETOR José Perelló Rafael

MALLORCA

SANTA MARGALIDA CA'N PICAFORT

CASAL SANTA EULALIA
Country hotel

Carretera Santa Margarita 24, 07450 Santa Margalida
Tel 971 18 5? 59 **Fax** 971 18 51 61

Yet another Mallorcan aristocrat's estate, this time more than 700 years old, which has been renovated over the last few years with no expense spared. The guest rooms and public rooms set a standard that can bear comparison with any on the island. They are full of light and furnished in a pleasantly minimalist fashion. Sandstone and wooden beams lend a discrete rustic charm. Morpheus, god of sleep, invites you to dream in antique beds and white bed linen. All the bathrooms are in beige marble; those in the suites are cavernous, and fitted with Jacuzzis. Throughout, *marès* stone is effectively used as a building material, even in the El Casal restaurant, a converted barrel vault, where modern art makes an interesting contrast with the fine furniture and rough surface of the sandstone. This is where to go if you want formal dining and quality Mallorcan cuisine.

The superb outdoor pool is in one of the most beautiful corners of the *finca*, reached by a path lined with palm trees. Here, the La Pedrera grill also familiarizes guests with fine Mallorcan cuisine, but in less formal surroundings.

Nearby Ca'n Picafort beach (1.5 km).
Location country road of Sta.Margalida-Alcudia, at the 6 km mark; garden and private parking
Food breakfast, lunch, dinner
Price €€€€, including breakfast, food €€-€€€
Rooms 25; 10 doubles, 11 junior suites, 4 suites, all with bath, central heating, air conditioning, telephone, hairdryer, satellite TV, minibar, safe
Facilities 2 restaurants, sitting room, bar, outdoor swimming pool, gym, sauna
Credit cards AE, MC, V
Children welcome **Disabled** no special facilities
Pets not accepted
Closed never
Manager Antonio Fiol

MALLORCA

SANTA MARIA

READ'S HOTEL
~ COUNTRY HOTEL ~

Carretera Vell Sta. Maria-Alaró s/n, 070 Santa Maria
TEL 971 14 02 61 **FAX** 971 14 07 62
E-MAIL readshotel@readshotel.com **WEBSITE** www.readshotel.com

THIS HOTEL'S ENGLISH OWNER, a former lawyer, has an entrepreneurial streak perhaps unusual in a 'safe' profession: more than a decade ago, Vivian Read bought an arid, flat piece of land, plus an old *finca;* it took six years' hard work to create his hotel, and now it is one of the best on the island. Palms have grown, and white parasols cast their shade around the enormous pool. Halls and corridors display an art collection gathered over 30 years. English Edwardian antiques rub shoulders with Victorian furniture, Sèvres china, sculptures and interesting old clocks. As you might expect, the furnishings of the comfortable suites and bedrooms are English rather than Mediterranean.

Food is served on an agreeable glazed-in veranda, with a pleasant temperature, looking out over a garden of several acres. Service can't be faulted. A spacious covered swimming pool was added in 1999, with sauna, whirlpool and solarium, so this is an all-year hotel.

~

NEARBY Santa Maria (3 km).
LOCATION edge of village; garden and private car parking
FOOD breakfast, lunch, dinner
PRICE €€€€, including breakfast, food €€-€€€
ROOMS 24; 8 doubles, 3 de luxe, 2 junior suites, 1 king and 1 princess suite, all with bath, central heating, air conditioning, telephone, hairdryer, satellite TV
FACILITIES restaurant, sitting rooms, bar, outdoor swimming pool, covered pool, gym, sauna, whirlpool, solarium, massage (on request), tennis court, bicycles
CREDIT CARDS AE, DC, MC, V
CHILDREN welcome if over 12
DISABLED no special facilities
PETS not accepted
CLOSED never
PROPRIETORS Vivian and Iris Read

MALLORCA

SÓLLER

CA'N AI
~ COUNTRY HOTEL ~

Cami Son Sales 50, 07100 Sóller
TEL 971 63 24 94 **FAX** 971 63 18 99

CONCEALED WITHIN A VAST ORANGE GROVE, surrounded by protecting mountains, the Ca n'Ai really is a real haven of peace, although the town of Sóller and the beautiful natural harbour of Port Sóller are only a few minutes' drive away. The former estate is surrounded by old walls and waterworks dating to the time of the Moors. *Sóllerics*, the natives of this area, refer to it as *el valle silensioso*, the valley of peace, and you'll notice the uncanny quiet as soon as you set foot in the garden.

The hotel offers suites only. Some incorporate galleries, either serving as a cosy little retreat, or housing the bath. The cheerful atmosphere, with whitewashed walls, wooden beams and pretty alcoves seems more Andalucian than Mallorcan. You will quickly feel at home, either in the cosy living room with its rocking chairs, or in the room with the open fire. The restaurant serves excellent, diverse dishes and locals eat here regularly.

~

NEARBY Sóller (2 km); beach (2 km).
LOCATION edge of town; garden and private car parking
FOOD breakfast, lunch, dinner
PRICE €€€€, including breakfast, food €€-€€€
ROOMS 11 suites, all with bath, central heating, air conditioning, telephone, hairdryer, minibar
FACILITIES restaurant, sitting rooms, outdoor swimming pool
CREDIT CARDS AE, MC, V
CHILDREN welcome
DISABLED no special facilities
PETS not accepted
CLOSED Nov-Jan
PROPRIETOR Domingo Morell

MALLORCA

SÓLLER

CA'N COLL
~ COUNTRY HOTEL ~

Cami de Ca'n Coll, 07100 Sóller
Tel 971 63 32 44 **Fax** 971 63 19 05

CA'N COLL IS JUST A FEW MINUTES from the centre of Sóller, on a hillside, in the middle of an orange plantation, and the *finca* enjoys splendid views on to the hills round about. The entrance hall, flooded with light, welcomes guests with certain Mediterranean aplomb. Bright cane furniture is offset naturally by terracotta-tiled floors; mahogany tables carry opulently stacked fruit bowls and overflowing flower arrangements; flower-patterned cushions artfully soften stone banquettes. A *trompe l'oeil* curtain across a passage makes an interesting talking point.

Rooms are airy and bright, with exposed pine beams providing an appropriately rustic look. In the large garden there is a swimming pool along with several sun terraces. Half-board is available on request. The food is excellent Mallorcan *cuisine*.

Sóller and its valley of orange plantations are a pleasant environment: the steep mountain slopes offer protection from the winds, which can be fierce, and the little town is a lively meeting place both for natives and visitors.

~

Nearby beach and harbour of Sóller (3 km).
Location 1 km from centre of Sóller; in garden and private parking
Food breakfast; dinner on request
Price €€€-€€€€ including breakfast, food €€
Rooms 8; 4 doubles, 4 suites, all with bath, central heating, air conditioning, telephone, hairdryer, satellite TV, safe
Facilities various sitting rooms, bar, outdoor swimming pool, bicycles
Credit cards MC, V
Children welcome
Disabled no special facilities
Pets not accepted
Closed never
Proprietor Emma Rodriguez

Mallorca

SÓLLER

Ca's Puers
~ TOWN HOTEL ~

Carrer Isabel II 39, 07100 Sóller
Tel 971 63 80 04 **Fax** 971 63 04 92
E-mail stay@caspuers.com

ONLY A FEW YEARS AGO, SÓLLER LAY HIDDEN among the orange orchards in the shade of the Tramuntana mountains. To get there, visitors had either to negotiate a winding pass – beautiful but difficult – or take the longer route via Valldemosa and Deià. Today, most holidaymakers reach the charming town the quick way, through an unromantic tunnel.

Ca's Puers is hidden away on one of Sóller's side streets, in an unprepossessing area. Only the large white sheet on the façade for protection against the sun indicates that something special goes on here. And indeed, the interior is unexpectedly grand: a wealthy local family lived here for many years, until its present German owner transformed it into one of Sóller's finest hotels. The six rooms are brightly furnished in a rustic-elegant style. Two delightful rooms, with the original decoration preserved, are used for intimate dining.

Austrian master chef Eckhart Witzigmann was lured here to take charge of the restaurant; depending on the weather, guests eat either on the glazed veranda or in the delightful garden. See page 125 in the restaurant section for a full review.

Nearby Port Sóller (4 km by tram); Fornalutx (5 km).
Location side street; private car parking
Food breakfast, lunch, dinner
Price €€€-€€€€, including breakfast, food €€€
Rooms 6; 5 doubles, 1 museum suite, all with bath, central heating, air conditioning, telephone, modem connection
Facilities restaurant, garden restaurant, sitting room, winter garden and terrace, private fishing boat
Credit cards AE, MC, V **Children** welcome
Disabled access difficult **Pets** not accepted
Closed Nov
Manager Britta Ploensgen

MALLORCA

SÓLLER

CA'S SANT
~ VILLAGE HOTEL ~

Cami de ses Fontanelles 34, 07100 Sóller
TEL 971 63 02 98 **FAX** 971 63 49 72
WEBSITE www.cas-sant.com

HIDDEN AMONG GREEN HILLS, BUT ONLY 800 M along a footpath from the centre of Sóller, lies the charming Ca's Sant. The scent of oranges wafts from the valley, and a fresh breeze blows from the natural harbour nearby.

A building, next door to the manor, houses four junior suites and a double room. Beautiful terracotta floors, and whitewashed walls combined with rough-cut stone, give the rooms a rustic feel. They are furnished with mahogany furniture from the early 19th century, including antique wooden chests. Rambles can be started right from the hotel.

A little railway runs from the centre of Sóller to the nearby harbour, Port Sóller. From there you can take a day cruise to the bays nearby, including the magical Sa Calobra ravine on the island's north coast.

In the vicinity of the hotel, and in the centre of Sóller, many elegant stone town houses dating from around 1900 are evidence of the new money that came here through the orange trade, and the return of newly enriched Mallorcans who had emigrated to France in order to improve their lot.

~

NEARBY Port Sóller (4 km).
LOCATION 800 m from the centre; in garden with private car parking
FOOD breakfast
PRICE €€€, including breakfast
ROOMS 5; 1 double, 4 junior suites, all with bath, central heating, air conditioning, telephone, hairdryer, minibar, satellite TV, safe
FACILITIES sitting room, outdoor swimming pool
CREDIT CARDS MC, V
CHILDREN welcome
DISABLED no special facilities
PETS not accepted
CLOSED never
PROPRIETOR Rafael Forteza

Mallorca
Sóller

Son Bleda
~ Country Hotel ~

Carretera Sóller a Deià s/n, 07100 Sóller
Tel 971 63 34 68 **Fax** 971 63 24 26
e-mail *info@sonbleda.de*

From Sóller the road snakes towards Deià, bringing you to the recently opened former manor house of Son Bleda. It was love at first sight for the two German owners when they set their eyes on this semi-ruin on a country road, with its incomparable view. They embarked on its restoration with a gusto that subsequently threatened to desert them, but now they can be proud of their persistence. Magnificent vases, a little fountain and thick old stone walls enliven the entrance. The cool, dark lobby is an inviting place in which to linger during hot weather. Breakfast is served here, prepared by the owners personally.

Rooms are in a 'modern rustic' style, with well-chosen antiques making useful statements here and there. Mind, body and spirit are pandered to in a room of ochre-coloured stone, where you relax in the whirlpool before a therapeutic massage.

Nearby Sóller (4 km); Deià (10 km).
Location on country lane; garden; limited parking
Food breakfast
Price €€€-€€€€, including breakfast
Rooms 9; 7 doubles, 2 suites, all with bath, central heating, air conditioning, telephone
Facilities whirlpool, chapel
Credit cards AE, MC, V
Children welcome
Disabled no special facilities
Pets small dogs allowed
Closed never
Proprietors Thomas von Hofe and Dieter Rahmel

MALLORCA

SON MACIÁ

SON MOLA VELL
~ FINCA HOTEL ~

Carretera Son Maciá–Calas de Mallorca, km 2, 07509 Son Maciá
TEL 971 55 46 64 **FAX** 971 55 56 17

You'll be captivated both by Son Mola Vell's position and pleasingly unpretentious architecture. The sand-coloured *marès* stone, typical of Mallorcan *fincas*, gives the estate much of its charm and character. Typical slatted windows, framed by pale-blue shutters, lend Mediterranean colour and atmosphere, as do the narrow cypresses. You are in the south-east of the island here, which still has much of Mallorca's old peace and charm, even in this era of mass tourism.

In the rooms, fine fabrics and tasteful furniture create a feeling of effortless comfort. They are average to generously sized, furnished in Mediterranean style. The food can claim to be memorable: a mixture of Mallorcan and traditional Spanish dishes includes delicious grilled artichokes with grains of coarse salt, sole cooked with capers and entrecote with apricots. There is a pleasant terrace where you can enjoy the timelessness of the scene over a sundown drink; or in chilly weather, indoors by the fire.

~

NEARBY Cala Romantica bay (5 km); Manacor (6 km)
LOCATION on the Son Maciá-Calas de Mallorca country road; own garden and private car parking
FOOD breakfast, dinner
PRICE €€€, including breakfast, food €€
ROOMS 10; 6 doubles, 1 single, 3 apartments, all with bath, central heating, air conditioning, telephone, hairdryer, satellite TV, minibar
FACILITIES restaurant, solarium, sauna, outdoor swimming pool, gym, tennis court (with floodlighting), 14-seater motor boat
CREDIT CARDS AE, MC, V
CHILDREN welcome
DISABLED no special facilities
PETS not accepted
CLOSED 1 Nov-20 Dec; 10 Jan-15 Feb
MANAGER Hubertus Schneider

MALLORCA

SON SUREDA

SON SUREDA
~ COUNTRY HOTEL ~

Carretera Manacor–Colonia de Sant Pere, 5.6km, 07500 Manacor
TEL 971 18 31 05 **FAX** 971 18 31 05

ABOUT SIX KILOMETRES FROM MANACOR, town of pearls, lies the 16thC *finca* of Son Sureda in the gently rolling countryside that is typical of the east of the island. It stands in grounds of some 200 hectares, surrounded by carob and almond trees, a Mediterranean forest and a botanic garden.

After extensive renovation, the rooms, some with open fireplace, have a homely, earthy character, and are ideal for families or small groups. Reclaimed olive wood has been used effectively for work surfaces in the apartments' kitchens. Walls are painted a sunny yellow and make a brilliant contrast to the rustic wooden furniture.

There are two fine swimming pools in the garden, so you won't be overcrowded as you cool off. If you like riding, this is the place for you: Spanish racehorses are bred on the estate and the owners will be pleased to tell you all about it.

~

NEARBY Manacor (6 km); Colonia Sant Pere beach (10 km).
LOCATION in own extensive grounds; ample private car parking
FOOD breakfast
PRICE €€-€€€, including breakfast
ROOMS 9; 5 apartments, 4 studios, all with bath, central heating, minibar
FACILITIES 2 outdoor swimming pools
CREDIT CARDS not accepted
CHILDREN welcome
DISABLED no special facilities
PETS not accepted
CLOSED never
PROPRIETOR Fernando Dameto

MALLORCA

SON TERMES

LOS NARANJOS
~ COUNTRY HOTEL ~

Cami Destre 61, 07120 Palma-Son Sardina
Tel 971 4? 90 00 **Fax** 971 43 84 83
E-MAIL hotel-naranjos@jet.es **WEBSITE** www.hotellosnaranjos.com

You can see the terracotta-coloured tower of the Los Naranjos estate from quite a distance – a significant landmark in its own right, and because it houses the hotel's finest set of rooms: a suite with a magnificent panorama over the valley, full of lusciously green orange trees.

This place is the dream of a German owner who has achieved a major transformation over several years. You enter through a heavy iron gate, along a narrow tree-lined road, to find an elegant, intimate country hotel, with just eight rooms, fitted out with every conceivable comfort. The interior design is Provençal rather than Mallorcan: cream-coloured sofas, armchairs, opulent fabrics, cherrywood furniture, elegant teak sunloungers with white upholstery, all bearing witness to a sophisticated design sense. The four-metre-long wooden table used for communal breakfasts and evening meals is a focal point, suiting best those guests who like a house-party atmosphere. The food is outstanding.

~

Nearby Palma (5 km); mountain village of Orient (15 km)
Location on the Palma-Sóller country road; garden and private car parking
Food breakfast, picnic baskets, dinner
Price €€€€, including breakfast, food €€€
Rooms 8; 5 doubles, 3 suites, all with bath, central heating, air conditioning, telephone, hairdryer, satellite TV, CD player, minibar
Facilities sitting-room, library, terraces, heated outdoor swimming pool, beauty farm, sauna, gym, solarium, massage, off-road vehicles, mountain bikes
Credit cards AE, MC, V
Children over 12 years welcome
Disabled no special facilities
Pets not accepted
Closed Nov
Manager Danielle van Dongen

MALLORCA

VALLDEMOSA

VISTAMAR
~ COUNTRY HOTEL ~

Carretera Valldemosa–Andratx, km 2.5, 07170 Valldemosa
TEL 971 61 23 00 **FAX** 971 61 25 83
E-MAIL info@vistamarhotel.es **WEBSITE** www.vistamarhotel.es

The road leading to the Hotel Vistamar is lined with magnificent trees, reminiscent of a scene from a Visconti film; and to sustain your sense of making a grand entry, four romantic pillars dominate the entrance. The building, dating from the late 1900s, and once the summer residence of the Fortuny family, is not in fact very large by the standards of the time, but the 19 bedrooms are enough to give 20thC guests a sense of space. (Twelve 'junior' suites have their own terraces.) They are decorated in the Mallorcan country style, with magical mahogany four-poster beds and local fabrics coming together effectively. The garden is a dream, with narrow paths leading down to shady romantic plateaux, which ask you to stop and read, or contemplate; or to admire the impressive view over Valldemosa's pretty harbour – a half-hour walk.

Valldemosa is associated with four famous people: the only Mallorcan saint, St Catalina Tomás; Archduke Ludwig Salvator of Austria; Frédéric Chopin and George Sand. The last two spent the winter of 1838-9 in the monastery at Valldemosa, having found no other lodging on account of Chopin's tuberculosis.

~

NEARBY Valldemosa (1 km); Deià (8 km).
LOCATION at the exit to the village in own grounds; ample private car parking
FOOD breakfast, dinner
PRICE €€€€, including breakfast, food €€
ROOMS 16; 5 doubles, 11 junior suites, all with bath, central heating, air conditioning, telephone, hairdryer, satellite TV, minibar
FACILITIES restaurant, sitting room, bar, outdoor swimming pool
CREDIT CARDS AE, MC, V
CHILDREN welcome
DISABLED no special facilities
PETS not accepted **CLOSED** Nov-Feb
MANAGER Pedro Coll

MENORCA

CALA MORELL

BINIATRAM
~ COUNTRY HOTEL ~

Carretera Cala Morell, 07760 Ciutadella
TEL 971 38 31 13 **FAX** 971 38 31 13
E-MAIL biniatram@infotelecom.es **WEBSITE** www.infotelecom.es

THE *FINCA* OF BINIATRAM ALREADY HAS 500 years of history under its belt. Like many villages and farms on the island beginning with 'Bini' (meaning 'sister of'), its name has its origins in Arabic and, therefore, of the Moorish occupation of southern Spain in the early Middle Ages – of which there are plenty of traces on all the Balearic islands.

This is a small 'farm' hotel, only a kilometre from the beautiful but crowded bay of Cala Morell, and it makes a pleasant, cool spot at the height of summer. The few rooms are simply decorated in country style, with a minimum of fuss and certainly no superfluous ornaments – which would not suit the style of the owners, who still farm the land, and are proud to do so. As a result, the atmosphere is homely, welcoming and relaxed. In the annexe, a fine room has been converted for celebrations, seminars and other events, also decorated in rustic style. The large kidney-shaped pool in the grounds is a refreshing oasis.

NEARBY Cala Morell (1 km); Ciutadella (4 km).
LOCATION on the country road to Cala Morell; garden and private car parking
FOOD breakfast
PRICE €€, without breakfast, food €
ROOMS 6; 4 doubles, 1 apartment with bedroom, 1 apartment with 2 bedrooms, all with bath, hairdryer
FACILITIES outdoor swimming pool, tennis court
CREDIT CARDS MC, V
CHILDREN welcome
DISABLED no special facilities
PETS by agreement
CLOSED 1 week in winter (enquire when booking)
PROPRIETORS Esperança Juaneda Benejam and
Joan Tomás Bagur

MENORCA

CIUTADELLA

HOTEL PATRICIA
~ TOWN HOTEL ~

Passeig de Sant Nicolas 90, 07760 Ciutadella
TEL 971 38 55 11 **FAX** 971 48 11 20
E-MAIL hotel@hesperia-patricia.com

THE PATRICIA IS ONLY A FEW minutes' walk from Ciutadella's wonderful old town, ideal for those who want action rather than peace. The comfortable rooms are furnished in a starkly modern fashion, nothing special, but equipped as you would expect in a properly run city hotel. A lavish buffet breakfast sets you up for the morning, and if you don't want to go to the beach, the inner courtyard has a swimming pool with large sun terrace. Guests have included the King and Queen of Spain.

Cuitadella is the starting point for tours of the neighbouring bays, and the harbour, lined with restaurants and cafés, has plenty of appeal. It's a good place to buy Menorcan cheese, little piles of which decorate many a shop window. (See also our entry on Sant Ignasi, page 92.)

NEARBY Cuitadella's centre (600 m).
LOCATION 400 m from the Plaça Conquistador; street parking in front of the hotel
FOOD breakfast
PRICE €€-€€€, including breakfast
ROOMS 44; 3 singles, 41 doubles, all with bath, central heating, air conditioning, telephone, hairdryer, satellite TV, minibar, safe
FACILITIES sitting room, bar, outdoor swimming pool
CREDIT CARDS AE, MC, V
CHILDREN welcome
DISABLED no special facilities
PETS not accepted
CLOSED never
MANAGER Xavier Vega

MENORCA

CIUTADELLA

SANT IGNASI
~ COUNTRY HOTEL ~

Carretera Cala Morell, 07760 Ciutadella
Tel 971 38 55 75 **Fax** 971 48 05 37
website www.santignasi.com

The road to this former *finca*, dating from 1777, leads past cultivated farmland and stables; it's a flat, sparse landscape, but in it is an oasis of evergreen oaks and palm trees, among which is hidden Sant Ignasi's ochre-yellow building, with its 20 rooms. The ten rooms on the *finca's* ground floor have access to a small private garden, where guests can breakfast in peace and enjoy a relaxed start to the day. Decoration of the public rooms, and the cosy bedrooms, is stylish and traditional. The restaurant spoils you with delicious Mediterranean food. An annexe close by offers a sauna, spacious terraces and a fine swimming pool.

The pretty harbour town of Ciutadella, only three kilometres away, has great shopping, cute little alleyways and the imposing Plaça Conquistador. Ferries leave the harbour for Mallorca (Cala Rajada, 90 minutes) and other destinations. (See also our entry on the Hotel Patricia, page 91.)

Nearby Ciutadella (3 km); Cala Morell beach (3 km).
Location northern outskirts of Ciutadella
Food breakfast, lunch, dinner
Price €€€-€€€€, including breakfast, food @@
Rooms 20; 18 doubles, 2 junior suites, all with bath, central heating, air conditioning, telephone, hairdryer, satellite TV, minibar
Facilities restaurant, sitting room, bar, outdoor swimming pool, sauna
Credit cards MC, V
Children welcome
Disabled no special facilities
Pets not accepted
Closed early Dec-early Jan
Proprietor Pedro Mayans

MENORCA

Es Castell

HOTEL ALMIRANTE COLLINGWOOD
~ TOWN HOTEL ~

Carretera de Villacarlos s/n, 07720 Es Castell
TEL 971 36 27 00 **FAX** 971 36 27 04 **E-MAIL** hotelalmirante@essa.net

THIS BEAUTIFULLY SITUATED terracotta villa looks more South American than Menorcan. Its heyday was the English occupation of Menorca, which lasted around 90 years, when Admiral Lord Collingwood resided here; but the building is in fact much older than that.

Now the English are here again, but this time as holidaymakers. The present owners acquired the dilapidated estate in the 1960s, renovated it and gave the whole thing that old-fashioned feel that appeals to the English – and the formula has worked.

In the winter of 2000-1, the bedrooms in the bungalows were fitted out with new furniture in Spanish country style. The entrance hall, public rooms and restaurant are altogether different, overflowing with old engravings and bric-à-brac, creating the impression that the admiral might still live here. There are a pool, tennis court, sun terraces and a restaurant.

~

NEARBY Mahó (2 km).
LOCATION 2 km from Mahó on the coast road to Es Castell, follow signpost on left to Es Castell; garden, private car parking
FOOD breakfast, lunch, dinner
PRICE €€, including breakfast, food €€
ROOMS 41 doubles, all with bath, telephone
FACILITIES restaurant, sitting room, bar, outdoor swimming pool, tennis court
CREDIT CARDS AE, MC, V
CHILDREN welcome
DISABLED no special facilities
PETS not accepted
CLOSED 30 Oct–1 Apr
MANAGER Enrique Pons Quintana

MENORCA

FERRERIES

SON TRIAY NOU
~ COUNTRY HOTEL ~

Carretera Cala Galdana 3, 07750 Ferreries
TEL 971 15 50 78 **FAX** 971 36 04 46

THE ROAD TO THE SON TRIAY NOU ESTATE is littered with sticks and stones, and runs past an endless dry-stone wall; but your journey will be brightened by the intense terracotta colour of the building, which comes into view from quite a distance.

There are just three guest rooms in the house, and a generously sized apartment in the annexe; so this really is a small hotel and an informal stay is guaranteed. The owners don't want to increase the accommodation with further conversions of estate buildings.

The elegant house looks more like a town villa than a farm, but farming is still practised here with all that that entails, including pigs and poultry. You'll have to get used to the strong country smells, but by the end of the first night we believe that you will have learned to cherish the special atmosphere of these simply furnished rooms. Enjoy the unique peace and quiet of the *finca* by the poolside or on a sunlounger: a real Menorcan idyll.

~

NEARBY Ferreries (3 km).
LOCATION open country; own grounds and car parking
FOOD breakfast, lunch, dinner
PRICE €€-€€€ including breakfast, food €€
ROOMS 4; 3 doubles, 1 apartment, all with bath, central heating, satellite TV
FACILITIES sitting room, outdoor swimming pool
CREDIT CARDS not accepted
CHILDREN welcome
DISABLED no special facilities
PETS not accepted
CLOSED never
PROPRIETOR Socorro Moisy

MENORCA

MAHÓ

HOTEL PORT MAHÓ
~ TOWN HOTEL ~

Fort de l'Eau 13, 07701 Mahó
TEL 971 36 26 00 **FAX** 971 35 10 50
E-MAIL portmahon@sethotels.com **WEBSITE** www.sethotels.com

MAHÓ IS MENORCA'S BUSY CAPITAL, and its harbour, Port Mahó, is of course one of its high spots, with the usual shoulder-to-shoulder restaurants, cafés and bars, all of which stay open late into the night.

The Port Mahó hotel, which is deep red with snow-white shutters, exudes an inviting, colonial sort of charm, and has an elevated position, giving a stunning view out over the harbour. Sadly, the elaborate and heavy revolving door is all that remains of the former *Art Nouveau* decoration, the place having been thoroughly converted to shining modern standards. The suites and rooms are unpretentious and tastefully furnished in an easy-living style. The restaurant is not well known, and you're probably best advised to steer towards the other restaurants and inns down on the harbour front, a mere five minutes' walk away. The large pool is definitely a highlight, as swimming in the harbour basin is far from ideal. The clientele includes yachtsmen on their way round the coast, who like to swap their rocking beds for a night on *terra firma*. A comfortable hotel for a short stay.

~

NEARBY harbour of Port Mahó.
LOCATION above the harbour; garden, private car parking
FOOD breakfast, lunch, dinner
PRICE €€-€€€€, iincluding breakfast, food €€
ROOMS 82; 73 doubles, 9 suites, all with bath, central heating, air conditioning, telephone, hairdryer, satellite TV, minibar
FACILITIES restaurant, sitting room, bar, outdoor swimming pool
CREDIT CARDS AE, MC, V
CHILDREN welcome
DISABLED no special facilities
PETS not accepted
CLOSED never
MANAGER Juan Olives Sintes

MENORCA

SANT LLUIS

ALCAUFAR VELL
~ COUNTRY HOTEL ~

Carretera Cala Alcaufar, km 7.3, 07710 Sant Lluis
Tel 971 15 18 74 **Fax** 971 15 14 92
E-MAIL info@alcaufarvell.com **WEBSITE** www.alcaufarvell.com

The MAGNIFICENT ALCAUFAR ESTATE, near Sant Lluis in the south-east of Menorca, is mentioned in local records as early as the 15th century. The changes that have affected other Balearic properties over the past few decades have to some extent passed Alcaufar by: agriculture and dairy farming still go on here, making it a great place for an authentic farm holiday.

Guests are lodged in the four rooms of the main house, where old family photos cover the walls. These, and tarnished mirrors, along with antique furniture (including wonderful *chaises longues* and fine mahogany beds) provide a glimpse into domestic life gone by on a Menorcan farming estate.

At 150 hectares, this is one of Menorca's largest estates. There's good walking and cycling on tracks through fields bounded by dry-stone walls, and the *finca* also owns a kilometre of coast, with one of the most beautiful sandy beaches on Menorca and crystal clear water. You can hire windsurfers (with tuition) or ride the horses.

~

NEARBY Mahó (6 km); Punta Prima beach (3 km).
LOCATION in open country; own grounds and car parking
FOOD breakfast; lunch and dinner on request
PRICE €€-€€€, including breakfast, food €€
ROOMS 4; 2 doubles, 2 junior suites, all with bath, hairdryer, satellite TV
FACILITIES room with open hearth
CREDIT CARDS MC, V
CHILDREN welcome
DISABLED no special facilities
PETS not accepted
CLOSED never
PROPRIETORS Maria Angeles and son Jaume de Olives

MENORCA

SANT LLUIS

BINIDALI
~ COUNTRY HOTEL ~

Carrer Suestra 50, 07710 Sant Lluis-Biniali
Tel 971 15 17 24; 971 35 41 28 **Fax** 971 15 03 52

You approach this hotel from Mahó via Sant Lluis along a charmingly Menorcan country road lined with an old dry-stone wall. (Sant Lluis is one of only seven villages on Menorca: only Ciutadella and Mahó count as towns.) The pretty building, surrounded by imposing palm trees, is in delightful countryside, but if you are expecting local design flair, think again. The owners, originally from Greece and Holland, can't do enough for their guests and have skilfully blended their own lifestyle with the layout of the house and the needs of guests. (Besides Greek and Dutch, English, Spanish and German are spoken here.)

Bedrooms are simply and tastefully furnished and decorated, and all have a bathroom. Some of the rooms have a generous terrace. From the large swimming pool you have a view to the sea. The cooking focuses on good, but plain and simple fare, and they'll prepare you a special dinner (or in summer a barbecue) on request. Both half- and full-board are available.

Nearby Cap de Font beach/bay (4 km).
Location on the country road 2 km from Sant Lluis in direction of Climent; garden and car parking
Food breakfast, lunch, dinner
Price €€-€€€, excluding breakfast, food €€
Rooms 11 doubles, all with bath, telephone
Facilities sitting room, outdoor swimming pool
Credit cards AE, MC, V
Children welcome
Disabled no special facilities
Pets not accepted
Closed 1 Nov-28 Feb
Proprietor Konstantinos Costas

MENORCA

SANT LLUIS

BINIARROCA
~ COUNTRY HOTEL ~

Carretera Es Castell-Sant Lluis, 07710 Sant Lluis
TEL 971 15 00 59 **FAX** 971 15 12 50
E-MAIL hotel@biniarroca.com

This romantic country hotel, a former 16thC estate comprising several buildings, lies in the triangle formed by the capital, Mahó, and the villages of Es Castell and Sant Lluis to its south. It's a typically Menorcan landscape, with dry-stone walls snaking their way through gently rolling countryside and edging the narrow lanes; the technique used for the walls' construction was brought to the Balearics by the Moors.

The property glistens like snow in the sun, its window frames and doors lacquered an aristocratic green. The entrance hall is decorated with opulent hangings, and on the walls there are flower paintings in oils by Lindsay Mullen that recall the French Impressionists, and which communicate the spiritual quality of the landscape. Rooms vary in size and decoration, but all have been individually and lovingly designed in a style reflecting the English charm of the owner, Sheila Ratliff. She creates an easy-going atmosphere that should enhance your time here.

The large pool and the sheltered pergola on the surrounding terrace are ideal for relaxation.

~

NEARBY Sant Lluis (3 km).
LOCATION well signposted on the Es Castell-Sant Lluis country road; own grounds and car parking
FOOD breakfast; lunch and dinner on request
PRICE €€-€€€, including breakfast, food €€
ROOMS 15 doubles and suites, all with bath, central heating, air conditioning, telephone, hairdryer, satellite TV
FACILITIES restaurant, sitting rooms, library, bar, 2 pools
CREDIT CARDS AE, MC, V
CHILDREN welcome
DISABLED no special facilities **PETS** not accepted
CLOSED Nov-Feb
PROPRIETOR Sheila Ratliff

IBIZA

IBIZA-TALAMANCA

OCEAN DRIVE
～ SEASIDE HOTEL ～

Platja de Talamanca, 07800 Ibiza
TEL 971 31 81 12

THIS MODERN DESIGNER HOTEL IS ONLY A minute's from the beautiful sandy beach of Talamanca, and from its terrace you have a view to the lively old town of Ibiza and its harbour, where many a crazy scene is played out. Despite the hotel's proximity to town and beach, it's a haven of peace, useful after a night on the town. There are more than 40 rooms, but the hotel has the feel of a much smaller place.

The German owner bought it in 1997 and rebuilt it as an Art Deco-style hotel, similar to those in Miami's Art Deco district. Bathrooms have cleverly-installed glass shower units, which make the rather small bathrooms look bigger than they are.

A substantial buffet is served in the inviting breakfast room, with its terracotta- and sand-coloured marble floor and white-upholstered chairs. There is no pool or garden, but that is no hardship, considering how close you are to the sea. The modern bar ('young modern' music, also 1920s-30s sounds) has a pleasant atmosphere.

～

NEARBY Ibiza (3 km)
LOCATION near Talamanca beach; own car parking
FOOD breakfast, set lunch, à la carte dinner
PRICE €€-€€€€€, including breakfast, food €€
ROOMS 42; 4 singles, 36 doubles, 2 suites, all with bath, air conditioning, telephone, hairdryer, satellite TV, minibar
FACILITIES restaurant, sitting rooms, bar
CREDIT CARDS AE, MC, DC, V
CHILDREN welcome
DISABLED no special facilities
PETS by arrangement
CLOSED never
MANAGER Albrecht Clari

IBIZA

IBIZA TOWN

LA TORRE DEL CANÓNIGO
~ TOWN HOTEL ~

Calle Mayor 8, Dalt Vila, 078001 Ibiza
TEL 971 30 38 84 **FAX** 971 30 78 43
WEBSITE www.elcanonigo.com

This hotel has been carved out of a 14th-century tower in Ibiza's upper town, but the harbour and the old town, the *Casco Antiguo*, with its many boutiques, bars and restaurants, are still accessible from here. The climb back up at night may not be for everyone; however, hotel guests are given a key to open the barrier that protects the old town from excessive traffic – so you can take your car up.

It's a charming place, with impressive old masonry everywhere, and well maintained. The eight suites come in various sizes, hence the wide range of prices. Some have the advantage of a terrace with a view over the old town, others overlook the courtyard. The largest are big enough for four and have a separate kitchen. The furnishings are rustic-influenced: lacquered iron beds with canopy and fine bed linen, and pretty decorative objects. There's a bar and a sitting room where drinks are served. Perhaps the most remarkable feature is the peace and quiet. Staff are attentive.

NEARBY centre and harbour (1 km).
LOCATION Ibiza's old town; street parking nearby
FOOD breakfast
PRICE €€€, including breakfast
ROOMS 8 suites, all with bath, central heating, air conditioning, telephone, satellite TV, minibar
FACILITIES sitting rooms, gym, sauna
CREDIT CARDS AE, MC, DC, V
CHILDREN welcome
DISABLED no special facilities
PETS accepted
CLOSED never
PROPRIETOR Javier Barcalzar

IBIZA

SANT MIGUEL

CA'S PLA
~ COUNTRY HOTEL ~

Apartado 777, Sant Miguel, 07800 Ibiza
Tel 971 33 45 87 **Fax** 971 33 46 03
E-mail hotel@caspla-ibiza.com

IBIZA TOWN IS ONE OF THE liveliest centres of the Balearic Islands; the old town in particular is a Mecca for nightbirds, voyeurs and tourists. Staying up until dawn and spending the day asleep on the beach is many people's object here, but for those who want to do exactly the opposite, there are a few hidden havens of peace and quiet; Ca's Pla is one of them.

It's a real gem: a former *finca* standing on a hill only a few metres from the beach and harbour of Sant Miguel, and surrounded by gnarled old pines, olives and carob trees. The Spanish style of decoration of the generous rooms is discretely highlighted with antiques, pictures and *objets d'art*. The bedrooms are painted in light colours and have a Mediterranean feel. There's a huge pool, surrounded by palm trees.

~

Nearby Sant Miguel harbour (2 km)
Location on country road heading towards Sant Miguel from Ibiza Town; garden and own car parking
Food breakfast; lunch and dinner on request
Price €€€-€€€€, including breakfast, food €€
Rooms 16; 4 doubles, 9 junior suites, 3 suites, all with bath, central heating, air conditioning, telephone, hairdryer, satellite TV, safe
Facilities restaurant, sitting room, bar, outdoor swimming pool, tennis court, bicycles, riding
Credit cards MC, V
Children welcome
Disabled no special facilities
Pets small dogs by arrangement
Closed 1 Nov-1 Mar
Proprietor Rosa Maria Natalia Sanchez

IBIZA

SANT MIGUEL

HACIENDA NA XAMENA
~ SEASIDE HOTEL ~

Na Xamena, 07815 Sant Miguel
Tel 971 33 45 00 **Fax** 971 33 45 14
website xamena@relaischateaux.com

Reached by one of the prettiest lanes on Ibiza, this hotel also enjoys one of the most fortunate locations on the island, surrounded by crags and pine woods. The terrace, around a large, curvacious swimming pool, hangs over a spectacular rocky cove which is accessible only by a scramble. (There are two more pools by the way, one indoors and heated.) The hotel is built in bright white Ibizan style, complemented by natural materials such as rocks and shady palm fronds, with many arches and rounded corners, and is arranged around a central patio. Solid chunks of wood and massive wooden beams create an impressive effect in the bar area. Bedrooms are on a lower floor, and each (except for single rooms) has a terrace or balcony and magnificent views. Some have whirlpool baths placed beside enormous windows directly overlooking the sea. The poolside restaurant, Las Cascadas, is ideal for sunset-watching and has an enviable local reputation. El Sueno de Estrellas, the other restaurant, is more intimate, and decorated in Moorish style.

A luxurious and secluded place in which to take refuge from the tourist traps of Ibiza, or from which to take guided hiking tours into the surrounding hills.

~

Nearby Sant Miguel (2 km).
Location near the sea; garden; parking
Food breakfast, lunch, dinner
Price €€-€€€, without breakfast, food €€€
Rooms 61; 52 doubles, 9 suites, all with bath, central heating, air conditioning, telephone, hairdryer, satellite TV, minibar **Facilities** 2 restaurants, sitting rooms, 2 outdoor swimming pools, covered swimming pool, tennis court, gym, sauna, fitness and beauty centre
Credit cards AE, MC, DC, V **Children** welcome **Disabled** no special facilities **Pets** allowed only in the rooms **Closed** 1 Nov-11 Apr
Manager Sabine Lipszyc

IBIZA

SANTA EULARIA

CA'N CURREU
~ COUNTRY HOTEL ~

Carretera Sant Carles, km 12, 07850 Santa Eularia
TEL 971 33 52 80 **FAX** 971 33 52 80
E-MAIL hotel@cancurreu.com **WEBSITE** www.cancurreu.com

This typically Ibizan *finca* lies in the heart of the island, surrounded by fig and orange trees, a mere 20-minute drive from Ibiza Town and a kilometre outside the picturesque little village of Sant Carles. Gleaming, whitewashed exterior walls are clothed in bougainvillea.

Inside, there are just five suites and two double rooms, all luxuriously fitted out, even with a kitchen. The design is typically 'Ibizan minimalist' – warm terracotta floor tiles, old wooden beams, white walls and bed linen – which exposes and emphasizes the building's structure instead of covering it up with kitsch. You probably won't use your kitchen much: the restaurant is the domain of one the finest chefs on the island, Carlos Posadas, highly regarded for his elegant, international dishes. The wine list is superb, too. A wonderful haven of peace and quiet on an otherwise busy holiday island.

NEARBY Cala Boix beach (2 km).
LOCATION on country road between Ibiza Town and Sant Carles; in garden with private car parking
FOOD breakfast; lunch and dinner on request
PRICE €€€€, including breakfast, food €€-€€€
ROOMS 7; 2 doubles, 5 suites, all with bath, central heating, air conditioning, telephone, hairdryer, satellite TV, minibar, safe
FACILITIES restaurant, sitting room, outdoor swimming pool, sauna, Jacuzzi, gym, solarium, horse riding
CREDIT CARDS MC, V
CHILDREN welcome
DISABLED no special facilities
PETS not accepted
CLOSED never
PROPRIETOR Vicente Mari Tur

IBIZA

SANTA GERTRUDIS

CA'S GASI
~ COUNTRY HOTEL ~

Cami Vell a Sant Mateu, 07814 Santa Gertrudis
TEL 971 19 77 00 **FAX** 971 19 78 99
E-MAIL casgasi@steinweb.net **WEBSITE** www.casgasi.com

As soon as you set foot in Ca's Gasi, you'll be bewitched by the scents wafting in from the surrounding land. The hotel is run by Margarete Martin von Korff, born in Barcelona but a citizen of the world - she worked for Lufthansa and spent four years going round the world on a boat. She puts a very personal stamp on it all, but it was never her ambition to run a hotel – opening up just seemed the obvious thing to do because the estate is so large. Guests get all the freedom and space they could need. There is no pressure, but whoever feels like it is welcome to participate in the preparation of meals and the everyday running of the hotel.

The elegant rooms are discretely furnished in a blend of country-house and oriental style. Shrimp-pink Venetian stucco gleams on the bathroom walls and Moroccan tiles decorate the fittings. Guests gather in a wonderful sitting room with an open fire for unforced get-togethers. Vegetables for the exquisite food are grown organically in the *finca's* garden. Another oasis of peace on this busy island.

~

NEARBY Santa Gertrudis (3 km).
LOCATION in open country; garden and own car parking
FOOD breakfast, lunch, dinner
PRICE €€€€, including breakfast, food €€
ROOMS 11; 9 doubles, 2 suites, all with bath, central heating, air conditioning, telephone, hairdryer, satellite TV, minibar
FACILITIES restaurant, sitting rooms, outdoor swimming pool
CREDIT CARDS AE, MC, V
CHILDREN welcome
DISABLED no special facilities
PETS not accepted
CLOSED never
PROPRIETOR Margarete Martin von Korff

EATING OUT

RESTAURANT SECTION INTRODUCTION

In the following pages we present 30 special restaurants in the Balearic Islands. This is quite a new departure for a *Charming Small Hotel Guide*, but one we hope to maintain in our smaller guides covering regions rather than whole countries. The restaurants follow exactly the same order as the hotels: first Mallorca, then Menorca and finally Ibiza.

What's the criteria for this selection? Simple – they are all noteworthy addresses, worth a journey, that we would like to pass on to our readers: places that our editor, who lives on Mallorca, has particularly enjoyed, and, of course, places that have the same quality of charm, individuality and value for money as the hotels that we recommend and which we know you appreciate. The majority are comfortable rather than luxurious, pretty and atmospheric rather than formal, with an emphasis on good regional cooking. A few are smart and expensive, but, in our opinion, worth it. We don't often stray into the territory of *haute cuisine* and three Michelin stars – it's not our style. Instead, these are the kind of places you dream of finding round every bend in the road: honest and welcoming, serving good food (it might be solidly traditional or subtly inventive) at fair prices.

The geographical distribution of our recommendations is entirely random: inclusion is based on the merits of the restaurant rather than popularity of a location, and many are in towns and villages where we do not happen to have hotel recommendations.

Finding a restaurant
Either browse through these pages, or use the Mallorca restaurant map on **pages 18-19;** restaurant locations on Menorca and Ibiza are combined with hotel locations in the location maps on **pages 20-23.**

Restaurant prices
As with our hotels, we have used price bands for the restaurants to indicate how much they cost. Restaurants vary widely in what they offer: some have just a couple of set menus; others offer menus ranging from cheap to expensive, plus an extensive *carte*. In devising our price bands we have calculated the cost of an average three-course meal for one person, without wine.

€	less than 10 Euros
€€	10-25 Euros
€€€	more than 25 Euros

MALLORCA

CALVIA

MESON CA'N TORRAT
~ VILLAGE RESTAURANT ~

Carrer Mayor 29, 07184 Calvia
TEL 971 67 06 82

SINCE THE COASTAL resorts of Peguera, Santa Ponça, Portals Nous and Illettes were incorporated into one large district, along with Calvia (which is the main town, with a population of approximately 2,000), this area has become the wealthiest in all Spain. That does not mean, however, that good restaurants grow on trees – quite the opposite, in fact. There are only four middling ones and one recommendable one: the Meson Ca'n Torrat, with its large covered terrace. The decoration is typically Spanish, typified by a bull's head hanging on the wall of the main room.

The kitchen produces delicious Spanish specialities, above all luscious meat dishes, making a starter almost superfluous. To take the edge off your appetite, rye bread with *aioli* (home-made mayonnaise with garlic) is brought to the table straight from the oven.

The *hors d'oeuvres* are highly recommendable, with delicious cooked and raw hams, home-made sausage and various cheeses from Mallorca and Menorca.

For your main course, the choice includes: *sopa de pollo* (chicken stew), piquant *frito Mallorqui;* vegetables and meat roasted together and served in the same dish including *conejo al ajillo* (rabbit on a bed of garlic), and the entrecôte steak, well-hung meat with scrumptious side dishes of aubergine, tomato and *zucchini*.

~

TYPE OF FOOD Spanish/local

OPENING TIMES 13.00-16.00 and 20.00-24.00; closed Thur

CREDIT CARDS MC, V

PRICE €-€€

Mallorca

Ciutat Jardi

El Bungalow
~ Seaside Restaurant ~

Carrer Arrecife 2, Ciutat Jardi
Tel 971 26 27 38

EL BUNGALOW IS A REAL RESTAURANT, although places such as this (known as *chiringuitos*) are normally closed out of season. Because of its position – the street behind the beach, with the sea right in front, and Palma nearby – it has become a favourite with the Mallorcans, so be sure to telephone in advance for a reservation.

The best atmosphere is around sunset, when you can sit on the terrace and simply have a drink with *tapas: pescaditos fritos* (small fried fish), *boquerones* (small fish marinated in vinegar and garlic) or *calamares*. Alternatively, take a seat in the large indoor room and eat the classic *chiringuito* dish: paella of various sorts. You could try the Valencian rice paella, made with shellfish, chicken and various vegetables, plus saffron-coloured rice cooked *al dente* – this goes well with a chilled rosé from the Penédés. For your main course, we recommend the delicious *fiduea negra*, expertly cooked. In a paella pan, seven-centimetre-long noodles, of spaghetti thickness, are tossed in oil with garlic and onion until golden yellow. Then *sepia* (cuttlefish) or small squid, still with their own ink, are added, followed by a little red wine. The dish is ready when the noodles have swollen, but are still *al dente*, and black as night. The fish dishes are also good, though rather dear, as everywhere else on the island. For pudding, the home-made *flan* (crème caramel) and *crema catalana* are excellent.

Type of food Spanish/local

Opening times Jun-end Oct 12.00-24.00, kitchen 13.00-16.00 and 21.00-24.00, Nov-May 13.00-18.00, Fri and Sat also evenings 20.00-23.30; Mon in Dec closed.

Credit cards MC, V

Price €€–€€€

MALLORCA

DEIÀ

ES RACO D'ES TEIX
~ VILLAGE RESTAURANT ~

Carrer de Sa Vinya Vell 6, 07179 Deià
TEL 971 63 95 01

IT'S SAD THAT THE PAINTERS AND SCULPTORS HAVE BEEN driven away from this former artists' village, mainly because of vastly inflated housing costs. To make up for it, however, culinary artists now hold sway, catering for a *coterie* of local gourmets with plenty of money to spend on dining out.

Coming from Palma, a narrow *cuesta* (gradient) leads behind the entrance to the village directly to this foodie's temple. The sun sets exactly opposite the low stone house in the summer months – a great sight, but you won't want it to distract from the food. The splendid terrace is a fitting stage for Joseph Sauerschell's performances: he has already earned a Michelin star at the El Olivo restaurant in the La Residencia hotel, Deià (see page 46) and is now trying to raise his profile even higher with his own venture.

The style of cooking is more *nouvelle cuisine* than international, but not like it was (ie large plates and tiny portions) in the 1970s. Sauerschell can claim to be the master of such delicacies as gently roasted juicy loin of lamb; vegetable pudding of artichokes; or perch served with goose liver in a sherry vinaigrette. Desserts are luxurious and – you would hardly expect otherwise – delicious. There's no question that for now, at least, prices are fair for what you get. As we went to price, this remained very much one of the island's hot tips.

~

TYPE OF FOOD modern Mediterranean

OPENING TIMES 13.00-15.30 and 19.30-23.30; closed Thur and Jan

CREDIT CARDS MC, V

PRICE €€€

Mallorca

Deià

Sa Vinya
~ Village restaurant ~

Carrer de Sa Vinya Vell 3, 07179 Deià
Tel 971 63 95 00

This restaurant, signposted on one of the stone walls of the main street and reached via a short climb, is further proof that masters of the culinary arts have replaced painters and sculptors in Deià (see also page 108). Klaus Goeggerle has created a distinctive atmosphere in the garden here, and on the flower-framed terrace, particularly in summer, where food is accompanied by jazz once a week.

For a starter, try the *langostinos con crema de aquacate* (giant prawns with avocado cream); or the crunchy salad with fried duck's liver. The fish soup is really quite creative, delicately flavoured with saffron and a splash of Pernod. For a main meat course, the *coneja borracho*, soused rabbit, is a delicious surprise: cut into matchsticks, seared and served with tagliatelle. For a rich fish dish, try the salmon in caviar cream with fine salad leaves and shrimp risotto.

Vegetarians will find wheat biscuits and various delicious vegetable noodles. The desserts are inventive, too: try fresh figs in *crème de cassis* or strawberries with basil sauce and vanilla ice cream. Maria's charming service adds to the experience.

~

Type of food international

Opening times 19.00-24.00; mid-Nov to mid-Feb closed on Thur

Credit cards MC, V

Price €€-€€€

Mallorca

Es Capdellà

Restaurant Bar Nou
~ VILLAGE RESTAURANT ~

Carrer Mayor 7, 07196 Es Capdellà
Tel 971 23 31 90

Es Capdellà, a modest village with narrow streets and pretty houses, has so far remained completely unspoiled by tourism and stands in stark contrast to Mallorca's tourist-filled coastal resorts. 'Nou' means 'new', and while it is true that this bar, and other small watering holes in the village, have been renovated in the past few years, it has been done without trying to emulate the chic tourist restaurants elsewhere. This is refreshing, and Bar Nou remains an unpretentious meeting place for the locals, and for cyclists touring the island.

Gambas, large prawns, are the house speciality. They are always eaten with the fingers, this being the best way to experience their full aroma. Equally recommendable is *pa amb oli*, literally 'oil with bread', appetizingly served with cheese from Mahó on Menorca, or with raw ham (or both). Juan, the chef, also makes delicious *albondigas*, little fish balls in a spicy sauce with salted potatoes. Equally good are the fried escalopes with a crunchy salad.

Ideal companions for the food are the wines from the nearby Santa Catarina vineyard, made from cabernet sauvignon and chardonnay grapes. (Every Sunday morning there are wine tastings in the vineyard's large dome-vaulted *bodega*, carved deep into the mountain.) For pudding, try the home-made lemon or almond cake. The service, provided mainly by family members and relatives, is friendly and attentive.

~

Type of food Mallorcan

Opening times kitchen 13.00-16.00 and 19.00-24.00; closed Wed and in Aug

Credit cards MC, V

Price €-€€

MALLORCA

ESTELLENCS

SON LLARG
~ VILLAGE RESTAURANT ~

Plaça Constitució 6, 07192 Estellencs
Tel 971 61 85 64

ESTELLENCS LIES ON A SLOPE IN THE SHADOW of Puig de Galatzo (1,025 m), among terraces of vines and vegetables. A short walk through the picturesque town, with its twisting alleys, stone houses and 500-year-old church of John the Baptist, is worthwhile before or after eating.

The Son Llarg restaurant is in the middle of the village, somewhat raised above the main street, thickly clothed with climbing plants; it spreads over two floors, and is furnished entirely in typical Mallorcan style, creating a cosy ambience.

The place is much admired by Mallorcans for excellent native cuisine. A good choice for a starter is the salad with stuffed eggs, the crunchy, fresh salad, or the selection of warm vegetables with paprika sauce. For main course, the lamb kidneys in sherry, cabbage stuffed with beef fillet in the Mallorcan style, and *conejo con cebollas* (rabbit with steamed onions) are excellent.

Along with wines from the island, such as Miguel Gelabert's splendid Riesling from Manacor, the Son Llarg also offers the Preludi de Raventos from the Penédes. If you prefer a red, try the Rioja Viña Pomal Reserva or the Pesquera from the Ribero del Duero estate. For dessert, the chocolate cake and the flambéed caramel pudding are outstanding.

Type of food Mallorcan

Opening times 12.00-15.30 and 19.00-22.30; closed Thur and 6 Jan to end Feb

Credit cards MC, V

Price €–€€

MALLORCA

GÉNOVA

NA BURGESA
Mountain restaurant

Cami Na Burgesa s/n, 07015 Génova
Tel 971 70 12 63

On the Na Burgesa, which towers 485 m above Palma to the south-west of the city near Génova, stands the eponymous statue of Mary: *Na Burgesa* (the town-dweller). The restaurant is reached on the Via Cintura (Palma's ring road), taking the Génova exit. On the way, make sure you take in the wonderful view over the city, the harbour and the cathedral of La Seu, as well as the broad arc of El-Arenal beach.

Likewise, try and get a table window in the restaurant for the breathtaking view. Unfortunately, you can't make a reservation, but it is worth waiting a while if all the tables are taken.

Wooden seats and wine racks create a rustic, cosy atmosphere. The menu combines both central Spanish and Mallorcan cuisine. Among the starters, the *frito Mallorqui* (quickly sautéed offal with vegetables) or snails (*caracols*) stand out, as do *conill amb cebas* (rabbit with onions) or crispy roast suckling pig among the main courses.

On the wine list, both the white and red Señorio de Sarria from Navarra are recommended with a clear conscience. After such a hearty meal, you may not want a pudding, so try instead a *Orujo Gallego*, a highly-prized spirit from northern Spain, with your coffee. Don't expect too much of the service: it is slow and not particularly friendly.

Type of food Spanish

Opening times 13.00-16.00 and 18.00-24.00; closed Mon

Credit cards V

Price €-€€

Mallorca

Palma

La Bóveda I and II
~ Town restaurants ~

Carrer Boteria 3/Passeig Maritim, 07012 Palma
Tel 971 71 48 63

PLAÇA LLOTJA IS DOMINATED BY THE IMPOSING, ecclesiastically inspired, 15thC maritime exchange, La Llotja. The building symbolizes Mallorca's former position as one of the Mediterranean's most important maritime powers. Today, it functions as an exhibition hall for the fine arts museum. This historic locality is also the site of two restaurants named La Bóveda: the original, in the Carrer Boteria, has an earthy atmosphere, where smoky walls and bulging barrels are the background to drinking and eating. The decoration of La Bóveda II, around the corner in the Passeig Maritim, is newer and more sober. There is a large terrace for open-air eating. Mallorcans avoid the place because of the crowds of tourists and the ever-rising prices.

A speciality of the Bóvedas is the *tapas*, available at the counter, in dishes such as *datiles con bacon*, dates mixed with fatty bacon and fried, *calamares en su tinta*, calamares cooked in their own ink, and *pimientos de padron*, tiny green peppers pan-fried and sprinkled with coarse sea salt just before serving. You should also try the *jabugo*, a delicious but expensive ham from southern Spain, produced from black pigs fed solely on acorns. A strong *Muga*, an earthy, full-bodied red Rioja, is the ideal accompaniment.

~

TYPE OF FOOD Spanish/local

OPENING TIMES 13.30-17.30 and 20.30-24.00; closed Sun

CREDIT CARDS AE, MC, V

PRICE €€

Mallorca

Palma

Chopin
~ Town restaurant ~

Carrer Puigdorfila 2 (Plaça Chopin), 07012 Palma
Tel 971 72 35 56

This stylish restaurant is adorned by a huge *trompe l'oeil* mural simulating a charming garden scene, but unfortunately, a disagreement with neighbours has resulted in the real garden, which was beautiful, being closed. Chopin is run by a Swiss couple, Pius Schneider and Gaby Fontana; he had a restaurant in Zurich that enjoyed a high reputation, just as Chopin does now.

The best of the appetizers include the cream of pumpkin soup and the consommé with ravioli. Among the main courses, the authentic Wiener schnitzel with potato salad is a winner. For this dish, a thin slice of veal (not pork, otherwise it would be a schnitzel in the Viennese *style*) is covered in fine breadcrumbs, fried golden brown, and garnished with lemon; a freshly drawn beer goes well on the side. Fish dishes, such as filleted ray, or the excellent monkfish, are wonderfully tender and well seasoned, but the side dishes are not particularly generous: two baby carrots and a courgette *coulis* can look a bit lost on the plate.

Wines are well chosen, though there are no exceptional or first-rate bottles on offer. *Crema Catalana* is an excellent dessert. Service is very attentive under Gaby Fontana's eagle eye. However, solitary guests who sit down at a table with a newspaper do not seem especially welcome.

The composer Chopin lived on Mallorca for a while, and you'll find his name used in various connections all over the island, not just here.

~

Type of food international

Opening times 13.00-15.30 and 19.00-23.00; Sat, evenings only, Sun closed.

Credit cards AE, MC, V

Price €€–€€€

MALLORCA

PALMA

LOS RAFAELES
~ TOWN RESTAURANT ~

Passeig Mallorca 28, 07012 Palma
TEL 971 72 62 40

THE LOS RAFAELES IS ONE OF THE FEW restaurants in Palma in which you can still come across Mallorcans, Spaniards and well-naturalized foreign residents. *Empresarios* (entrepreneurs) and *funcionarios* (high-ranking officials) sit with their colleagues and friends in orderly groups at the bar or at the white-covered tables, where they are served by attentive *camareros* (waiters). Unlike in the rest of Spain, the main meal of the day is eaten here at midday.

Behind the counter, delicious *tapas* – a mixed platter is the house speciality – are neatly arranged with a slanting mirror behind, in order to enhance their display. There are *piminetos de padron*, tiny green peppers sautéed and sprinkled with coarse sea salt prior to service (as are the artichokes cut in strips), freshly-caught shrimps, squid, anchovies, *croquettes* and salads.

Among the main dishes, the perch is wonderful, and the side dishes are typically Spanish: chalk-white potatoes (tasting of nothing much), and vegetables. The small lamb cutlets flavoured with rosemary are beautifully pink, and substantial enough to make a filling dish. For dessert, we recommend the lemon mousse, and the Mallorcan pudding (served as a thick rectangular slice and topped with caramel sauce).

~

TYPE OF FOOD Spanish/local

OPENING TIMES 13.00-17.00 and 20.00-23.00; closed Sun

CREDIT CARDS MC, V

PRICE €€

MALLORCA

PORT D'ANDRATX

MIRA MAR
RESTAURANT BY THE HARBOUR

Avenida Mateo Bosch 22, 07157 Port d'Andratx
Tel 971 67 16 17

A PLACE IN WHICH TO SEE AND BE SEEN. You can eat on the terrace under an awning, with a grandstand view of marina, harbour basin and fishing boats, secure in the knowledge that this restaurant is a classic: you are guaranteed first-rate food, friendly service and a cultivated ambience.

As a starter, you should try the delicious *sobrasada*, a house speciality: peppered smoked sausage, which is made here with added honey. A strange mixture, you may think, but it's delicious. Also worth trying are the salad of lightly sautéed *alcachofas* or *espárragos* (artichokes or green asparagus). In between, or as an accompaniment, *pommes alumettes*, shredded, fiercely sautéed potatoes, are simply delicious.

For your main course, you should try either the *dorada a la sal*, John Dory in a salt crust, or a *cassoleta de peix*, a casserole of various fish in a hearty sauce. The fish is always fresh, almost straight from the boats. Equally recommendable is an *arròs negre* (black rice or black paella), in which small squid are cooked in their own ink with garlic and onions.

From the wine list, try a white Herederos Ribas from Binissalem or the red Rioja, Conde de Valdemar Reserva 1997. For dessert, the Mallorcan almond ice cream (*helado de almendras*) or almond cake (*gató de almendras*) are excellent.

Type of food Spanish

Opening times 12.00-16.00 and 19.00-24.00; closed 15 Dec-15 Jan

Credit cards AE, MC, V

Price €€-€€€

MALLORCA

PORT D'ANDRATX

EL PATIO
~ ROADSIDE RESTAURANT ~

Carretera Andratx-Puerto, km 20, 071057 Port d'Andratx
TEL 971 67 20 13

EL PATIO STANDS RIGHT on the busy road from Andratx to Puerto, but inside the atmosphere is refined and peaceful – possibly a reflection on the quality of the staff, but also because of the old farmhouse's thick stone walls. The clientele is predominantly German; summer visitors from nearby Port d'Andratx, and they seem to accept with equanimity the long waiting times for the food and the rather high prices. There's a huge patio – hence the name.

The menu, meanwhile, can claim to be classic, at least in this type of restaurant. Among the entrées, potato-truffle ravioli with freshwater crabs, or the *carpaccio* of turbot, are excellent. For a main course you can choose from refined creations such as rabbit stuffed with lobster on a bed of orange and tarragon; red mullet with tomato *confit*; or sweet and sour breast of duck.

The well-chosen wine list is restricted to fine vintages, so be prepared to pay a price. Desserts – labour-intensive concoctions that use a wide range of ingredients – also come with a price tag. But the chef really does know what he's doing, and by this time the cost probably won't deter you because you'll be feeling that all is well with the world.

~

TYPE OF FOOD international

OPENING TIMES 19.30-23.30; closed Mon and from Nov to the middle of Mar

CREDIT CARDS MC, V

PRICE €€€

Mallorca

Port de Pollença

Restaurant Stay
~ Harbour restaurant ~

Carrer Muelle Nuevo s/n, Port de Pollença
Tel 971 86 40 13

It was the British who discovered Pollença, and Port de Pollença, at the turn of the 20th century. The little fishing village, with its 2,100 inhabitants, extends picturesquely along its bay; despite the throng of tourists, it has retained its character, and there are no high-rise hotels here. Perhaps the name of the restaurant was chosen mainly in honour of the English clientele. It is situated on the breakwater and has a panorama over the harbour, beach, sea and the mountains behind. Guests sit on a glazed terrace or, in good weather, directly by the sea.

The food is excellent, produced only from fresh ingredients, and presentation is impressive. As a starter you should try *ensalada mixta Stay*, made with various greens, chicory, avocado, fresh artichoke hearts, delicious tomatoes and a thickened vinaigrette. There is also *parrillada de verduras con salsa de romesco:* a mixture of lightly sautéed vegetables and oyster mushrooms, accompanied by a delicious sauce made from dried red peppers, almonds, garlic and herbs pounded in a mortar with olive oil. Or there is *tartar de pescado*: fresh, raw fish blended into a piquant mayonnaise; or you could try ravioli filled with partridge in a delicate wild mushroom sauce. For a main course, you're probably best with the fish, which is freshly caught, displayed on ice in the cabinet, and served *a la plancha* (grilled). Service is effective and friendly.

~

Type of food Spanish

Opening times 12.30-16.30, Fri and Sat, 15 Mar-31 Oct; also evenings 19.30–23.30

Credit cards MC, V

Price €€-€€€

MALLORCA

PORTOCOLOM

COLON
~ HARBOUR BISTRO-RESTAURANT ~

Carrer Cristobal Colon 7, 07670 Portocolom
TEL 971 82 47 83

THE HOURS SEEM TO PASS SLOWER IN PORTOCOLOM than elsewhere on Mallorca. People saunter leisurely through the village, or while away time in street cafés, or on the terrace of the Colon bistro-restaurant, which is one of the area's main assets.

The idea for this gourmet temple, furnished in the style of the American Deep South, came from Nona von Haeften, who for several years has run an interior design shop in Manacor, and Wolf Siegfried Wagner. Dining here, you could indeed feel as if you were on a southern plantation, or perhaps in an African safari lodge. Big fans circulate the air, often helped by a cool breeze from the harbour.

The chef is Dieter Sogner, whose work has taken him far and wide; he trained in Munich at the Tantris with Alfons Schuhbeck and Hans Haas.

Sogner is recognized for refined, delicate creations. To begin, try the delicious *carpaccio* of swordfish or mussels on marinated lentils. If you want fish as a main course, the monkfish on a celery purée is excellent; if meat, try pink lamb in red wine with a mushroom *roulade*. Among the desserts, you won't forget the rhubarb tart with champagne jelly. Service, provided by Sogner's wife, Onika, is attentive and patient.

~

TYPE OF FOOD international

OPENING TIMES Bistro from 12.00 onwards, restaurant 13.00-15.30 (except Aug) and 20.00-23.30; closed Wed and mid-Jan–mid-Feb

CREDIT CARDS MC, V

PRICE €€€

MALLORCA

PUERTO PORTALS

FLANIGAN
~ HARBOUR RESTAURANT ~

Plaça del Puerto, 07181 Puerto Portals
TEL 971 67 61 17

PUERTO PORTALS, ONCE AN UNSOPHISTICATED fishing village, now has luxury yachts in the harbour basin; elegant folk on the promenade, and attention-grabbing cars thundering past its many restaurants and cafés. Flanigan is one of the best, perhaps *the* best, and it's unusual among restaurants on the island for not closing at midday. The King and Queen of Spain are regular patrons.

For starters, the finely sliced, extremely delicate *jabugo* ham (from black pigs) is appetizingly presented. For a main course, the Mallorcan *tumbet* is worth a try; made of aubergines, *zucchini*, onions and tomatoes, it is similar to the French *ratatouille*, and considered best when eaten with fillet of beef. The marvellous house hamburger is an old favourite: don't be embarrassed to order one, it's far from taboo. On the fish menu, the finest sea creatures turn up daily, from small prawns in olive oil with garlic, to sole and sea bream; all are well prepared and presented. Red meat eaters will appreciate the steaks, accompanied by gratinée potatoes and good vegetables.

The wafer-thin apple cake is a delicious dessert, made to order, which takes 20 minutes, so think ahead if this is your choice. Service is average, with adequate numbers of not-very-professional staff. The owner prefers diners who speak Spanish.

~

TYPE OF FOOD Spanish/international

OPENING TIMES daily 10.00-24.00, kitchen 12.00-23.00

CREDIT CARDS MC, V

PRICE €€-€€€

Mallorca

Puigpunyent

Sa Tafona Son Net
~ COUNTRY HOTEL RESTAURANT ~

Possessió Son Net, 07194 Puigpunyent
Tel 971 14 70 00

THE RESTAURANT HAS BEEN CREATED IN THE *TAFONA*, the old oil mill, of a former 17thC estate. The walls are almost 10 m high, and the interior is dominated by mill stones and imposing wooden beams. It has a fabulous panorama of the surrounding mountains and valleys.

The Mallorcan Xisco Martorell has been established as head chef at Son Net for a while now, having cut his teeth at the El Olivo in Deià (see page 46) and in the Ca n'Ai in Sóller (see page 81). He delights guests with fresh produce from Mallorca and the mainland.

For starters, try the lukewarm *ensalada templada de langostinos y calamares* or the grilled vegetables with the delicious Sóller oil. A memorable fish dish is the *San Pedro a la sal*, monkfish baked in a salt crust that keeps the fish tender and juicy, accompanied by a ragout of chick peas and other vegetables and *sobrasada*, the typical Mallorcan sausage. An outstanding meat dish is *carré de cordero con crosto de queso Mallorquin*, loin of lamb in a Mallorcan cheese crust.

If it's a special occasion, treat yourself to a bottle of Jean Leon, a 1980 cabernet sauvignon; if you're on a budget, stick to the Conde de Valdemar Rioja. For dessert, definitely try the *tarta de manzana*, a warm apple cake served with rum and raisin ice cream, or *tejas de pan de miel con clementinas Mallorquinas*, a delicate shortcrust tart filled with honey.

~

Type of food international

Opening times daily 13.00-16.00 and 20.00-23.30

Credit cards AE, DC, MC, V

Price €€€

MALLORCA

RANDA

ES RECÓ
~ COUNTRY HOTEL RESTAURANT ~

Carrer Font 13, 07629 Randa
Tel 971 66 09 97

E**s reco is splendidly** sited on a hill between two mountains, with a spectacular view as far as Palma. Before or after eating, you can take a pleasant walk through a pine wood up to the 15thC monastery complex of Santuiri de Sant Honorat.

The speciality here is refined but simple Mallorcan fare, and you would do well to order a full range. For example: first course, *sopa de almendras*, almond soup, with its novel taste. Second course: *frito Mallorqui*, a selection of vegetables and very finely chopped offal, sautéed in a pan. Third course: *lubino a hinojo silvestre*, perch in a fine fennel sauce. Next, a small home-made lemon sorbet as palate-cleanser, then, as the fourth course, *cochinillo asado al horno de leña*, suckling pig roasted in a wood-burner with delicious garlic potatoes and sweet green beans. Fifth course: *helado de almendras con gató*, home-made almond ice cream with the typical almond cake of the island.

Also highly recommended is the salad of avocado, apple, sweetcorn, baby carrots, and tomatoes, dressed with a delicious vinaigrette. The wine cellar is well stocked; one of several delights is the local dry muscat, the Miguel Oliver from Petra. A small plate of glacé walnuts, chocolate truffles and almonds is offered with coffee. Best to book in advance.

~

Type of food Spanish/local

Opening times daily, 12.30-16.30 and 19.30-23.30

Credit cards AE, MC, V

Price €€-€€€

MALLORCA

SANT TELM

CALA CONILLS
~ RESTAURANT BY THE SEA ~

Cala Conills 42, 07159 Sant Telm
TEL 971 23 91 86

Sant Telm, at the southern tip of Mallorca, only really comes to life in summer, when, among other things, people come here to make the trip across to the island of San Dragonera in the *Santa Margarita*, a large fishing vessel. There are plans to make a larger marina, which will surely spell the end of any peace which the locals enjoy out of season.

The spectacular position of the Cala Conills matches the exceptional service and the charming smiles of the owner, Maria, who writes up the dishes of the day on a huge board. You sit in the shade of a straw canopy. The rock on which the terrace has been built gives almost directly on the water, with only the sea-water swimming pool between. This is a life saver on hot days: it's a difficult descent to the sea over precipitous rocks.

The best thing to eat here is fresh fish. The choice ranges from sardines, simply grilled, to turbot, perch, prawns and sole. For red meat enthusiasts there is a sensational *solomillo con salsa de pimienta* (fillet steak with fresh peppercorns). From the dessert list, the *tiramisu* is an absolute dream and the *carajillo* (black coffee with a shot of brandy) the perfect companion.

The wine list is well chosen and lively, including a Viña Sol de Torres, popular with the Germans, but by no means outstanding.

~

TYPE OF FOOD Spanish/local

OPENING TIMES 10.00-24.00; closed Nov-Apr

CREDIT CARDS MC, V

PRICE €€-€€€

MALLORCA

S'ARRACÓ

LA TULIPE
∼ VILLAGE RESTAURANT ∼

Plaça de Toledo 2, 07159 S'Arracó
TEL 971 67 14 49

ACCORDING TO A TOURIST GUIDE published at the turn of the 20th century, the journey from Palma to S'Arracó took about nine hours by donkey cart. Today, the journey by car is almost too fast to enjoy the countryside on the way; however, it's worth making, if only for this restaurant.

Behind the jaunty façade lies a delightful, tasteful restaurant offering healthy, mainly vegetarian food. Service from Brigitte, the Swiss co-owner, is exceptional. In the front part of the restaurant, a mural by the Catalan painter Pepe Suari defines the space.

The Swiss chef René cooks exceptionally tasty, international-Mediterranean dishes. The *à la carte* menu changes four times a year, and the daily menu every two weeks, so it is quite possible that the dishes described here will not be available. When our author visited, the *carpaccio* of vegetables with lukewarm vinaigrette, and the leaf salad garnished with goat's cheese, were excellent. Among the main courses, so was the beef fillet with morel sauce, and the breast of guinea fowl on a grape sauerkraut. The chef understands everything about fish, and the pan-fried or grilled monkfish is superb. From the wine list we recommend the red or white house wine; the local Jaume Mesquida; or Muga, a very drinkable red Rioja. From the desserts, the *crema Catalana* is up there with the best.

∼

TYPE OF FOOD international/Mediterranean

OPENING TIMES from 19.30; closed Sun in Jul and the first weeks in Dec

CREDIT CARDS MC, V

PRICE €€-€€€

MALLORCA

SÓLLER

CA'S PUERS
~ TOWN HOTEL RESTAURANT ~

Carrer Isabel II 39, 07100 Sóller
TEL 971 63 80 04

SÓLLER HAS SEEN MAJOR IN CULINARY DEVELOPMENTS in the last few years. The opening of a tunnel has made the little town more accessible, stimulated restaurant trade, and opened up choices, one of which is the hotel-restaurant Ca's Puers: for a review of the hotel side of the operation, see page 83 in the Mallorca hotel section.

The food is under the overall direction of the Austrian star cook Eckhart Witzigmann (if he is on the island), who recently extended his reputation by contributing to a vegetarian cook book. In day to day charge of the kitchen is the young Roland Trettl, and he does not disappoint.

For a delicate starter, try the *calamares cannelloni* with salad and Serrano ham, or the pearl barley risotto with *petits pois*, Serrano ham and *boletus* mushrooms. For a main meat or fish course, recommendable options are saddle of lamb with roast courgette flowers; and braised devil fish, accompanied by tuna, tomatoes and olive *gnocchi*. The wine list is well chosen; even the wines sold by the glass are excellent. Puddings consist of variations on yoghurt, rhubarb and lemon.

Near to the Ca's Puers, only a few minutes from the town centre, the Ploensgen family has opened a second hotel-restaurant, the Ca's Xorc, in a town house with small garden and glazed-in terrace.

~

TYPE OF FOOD International

OPENING TIMES 19.30-24.00, Sat and Sun also 13.00-16.00; closed Mon

CREDIT CARDS AE, DC, MC, V

PRICE €€€

MENORCA

CIUTADELLA

CAFÉ BALEAR
～ HARBOUR RESTAURANT ～

Lago Cala'n Bosch, 07760 Ciutadella
TEL 971 38 00 05

CIUTADELLA IS A TOWN WITH A RICH HISTORY, interesting architecture and friendly people, well worth a visit, especially if combined with eating at The Café Balear. It's not, in fact, a café, but one of the best restaurants on Menorca. You reach it by a long stone staircase that leads down from the imposing Plaça Conquistador to the harbour.

The decoration is stolid, as indeed is the atmosphere in the early evening, when the first guests are mainly foreign visitors. The locals, and the Spaniards, prefer to dine later in the evening, and then the mood becomes much livelier.

As an entrée, try the *salpicon* (seafood salad) or *sopa de pescado* (fish soup). For main courses, there's a wide choice – as the Spanish seem to demand. You'll find *lubina al sal* (pike in a salt crust), anointed with barely melted butter; or *rodaballo a la plancha* (grilled turbot).

The wine list is well chosen, with Reservas de Pesquera, wines from the Ribera del Duero and fine vintages from Rioja.

～

TYPE OF FOOD Spanish/local

OPENING TIMES 13.00-16.00 and 19.00-24.00; closed Mon and two weeks in Nov

CREDIT CARDS MC, V

PRICE €€-€€€

MENORCA

Mahó

PASARELA
∼ Harbour restaurant ∼

Andén de Poniente 25, 07701 Mahó
Tel 971 36 68 71

The Pasarela enjoys a fabulous position on the second largest natural harbour in Europe. Its marine-blue sun awning is the ideal vantage point from which to gaze at the comings and goings on the water: large cargo and passenger ships come right up to the town, among them ships of special interest such as *Royal Clipper*, the world's only five-master ship, modelled on the legendary German *Prussia*, which caused quite a stir when she visited in 1999.

The restaurant's decoration is somewhat conventional, but the food has what it takes. The menu is varied: you have a choice of five starters and main courses. Among the former, the *almejas en salsa verde* (mussels in green sauce) are very recommendable, as are the shellfish salad or the mussels *a la marinera*.

As you would expect, paella is offered; there's a good mixed one, combining meat and shellfish. If you are interested in local fare, try the delicious loin escalope with Menorcan cabbage. Included in the set menu price is bread, wine or water, dessert and VAT.

∼

Type of food Spanish/local

Opening times 12.00-16.00 and 19.00-24.00; closed Jan and Feb

Credit cards MC, V

Price €€

Menorca

Mahó

Portobello
∽ Harbour restaurant ∽

Andén de Levante 218, 07701 Mahó
Tel 971 35 43 60

The popular Portobello immediately grabs your attention, not just because of its yellow sun awning, but because of its unique position. You can usually get a table straight away on the large terrace, but when things are busy, it is worth waiting, because this is a great place for people- and yacht-watching.

The menu is 'international fusion', but definitely aimed at the predominantly English clientele. There are a few surprises, however, as the chef has served his time – and learnt a great deal – in a variety of restaurants. Hence the *spaghetti napoli*, with a first-rate tomato sauce that would be the envy of any Italian chef. Crunchy salads are served with dressings and are all delicious. The universally popular *entrecote*, elsewhere hastily prepared and usually rather tough, is the exact opposite at Portobello, again just right for the English diners.

∽

Type of food international

Opening times daily, 10.00-24.00

Credit cards MC, V

Price €€

MENORCA

MAHÓ

LA SIRENA
~ HARBOUR RESTAURANT ~

Andén de Levante 199, 07701 Mahó
TEL 971 35 07 40

VERA AND WALTHER GRAAB TOOK A GAMBLE with the Sirena, but it has paid off. Before coming here, Walther was a chef in Greece, Madeira and Switzerland, and favours healthy eating, using fresh, organically grown produce from the island. This is somewhat daring in a country of dedicated meat eaters; but support for health-conscious food is growing even here. The restaurant occupies a good position on the harbour front, and consists of a narrow room with the bar and kitchen to one end, and is simply decorated. In summer, the best place to be is the terrace.

Vera greets you with olives, *aioli*, bread and red wine. Then comes the *tuareg* salad with warm goat's cheese melting on to the leaves, as popular with the regulars as the mixed Arabic *hors d'oeuvres*, including, of course, *falafel*, little deep-fried balls of delicately spiced chick pea purée. Excellent main courses include the wholewheat spaghetti with a pesto sauce; tagliatelle with strips of smoked salmon; *zucchini* in a first-rate cream sauce; and carrot tagliatelle in more cream, accompanied by freshly grated potato cakes fried a golden brown, and delicious *boletus* wild mushrooms.

TYPE OF FOOD international

OPENING TIMES 19.00-24.00, in winter also 12.00—16.00 Thur to Sun; closed Tue and 2 weeks in Jan

CREDIT CARDS MC, V

PRICE €€

MENORCA

SANT CLIMENT

CA'N BERNAT
~ COUNTRY RESTAURANT ~

Carretera Climent-Cala'n Porter, 07712 Sant Climent
TEL 971 37 72 94

THIS CONSPICUOUS LITTLE WHITE HOUSE on the Climent-Cala'n Porter country road seems to possess some unseen influence, drawing in visitors from afar. (To reach it, branch off on the road to Son Vitamina.) This is a family business, with cordial and prompt service – book well in advance if you want to go at a weekend.

As you walk into the restaurant, you meet a seductive aroma of fresh meat barbecued with a sprinkling of rosemary. On the terrace, sheltered from the sun, clients sit with expectant faces. The chef walks across to the grill carrying a huge tray laden with T-bone steaks, fillets and spare ribs. – for which the restaurant is (at any rate locally) well known. Before getting into these, you can have an appetizer of addictive *aioli*. If you don't want the barbecued meat, there's grilled rabbit with crispy potatoes and a crunchy side salad. The spare ribs are perfect – dark brown on the outside and moist on the inside, served with an excellent ketchup. A particularly good side salad with ripe tomatoes and sweet onions combines well with the red meat dishes.

If you still want to eat a dessert, try the truly delicious homemade *flan*.

~

TYPE OF FOOD Spanish/local

OPENING TIMES 11.00-16.00 and 19.00-24.00; closed Tue, Jan and Feb

CREDIT CARDS MC, V

PRICE €€

IBIZA

IBIZA TOWN

EL BRASERO
~ TOWN RESTAURANT ~

Carrer Es Passadis 4, 07800 Ibiza Town
TEL 971 31 14 69

THIS RESTAURANT IS AN INSTITUTION, patronized by a sophisticated band of international regulars from the worlds of fashion and cinema.

After an excellent meal, you sit in El Brasero as if in the front row of the stalls, in order to observe the street scene enacted before you every evening in summer. Around midnight, groups of people dressed up in party clothes trail through the old town, wearing clothes advertising the names of the town's discothèques, and having plenty of fun in the process: a vivid, strange masked ball of semi-naked bodies.

The menu offers French-inspired international dishes. Starters include a delicious salad of warm goat's cheese, or a *salad Niçoise*. Eating fresh fish for the main course is a point of honour here: you have a choice of John Dory, bream or sole. Red meat eaters will be satisfied with the lamb or beef fillet. The wine list is well chosen, if expensive. For pudding, the home-made *flan* and the *crema Catalana* are recommended.

~

TYPE OF FOOD French/international

OPENING TIMES 20.30-24.00, in winter 19.00-24.00; closed Mon and Tue and 15 Dec-15 Feb

CREDIT CARDS MC, V

PRICE €€€

IBIZA

IBIZA TOWN

EL CORSARIO
~ TOWN RESTAURANT ~

Carrer Ponent 5, 07800 Ibiza Town
TEL 971 30 12 48

THIS IS AN IBIZAN LEGEND. When the island was being discovered by the hippies in the 1960s, and the Guardia Civil were gazing through binoculars at the first topless (or even naked) bodies among the sand dunes on Las Salinas beach, guests were already staying at the El Corsario. Brigitte Bardot often spent her holidays here, plus entourage. The hilltop house was a refuge for corsairs in the 17th and 18th centuries, but today it is a top-class hotel and restaurant under the direction of Beatrice Heppe. From the terrace you have a clear view over the old town and the harbour, indeed of almost the whole island.

Austrian chef Alexander Bulla holds sway in the restaurant. He trained with Eckart Witzigmann and Heinz Winkler, who ran the Tristan gourmet restaurant on Mallorca for more than 15 years. Bulla, ambitious to emulate the success of his mentors, is eagerly striving for the first Michelin star on Ibiza, and he's in with a chance.

The consommé of celery makes a superb entrée. Try following it with wild salmon in a tomato jelly and caviar; or delicately steamed wolf-fish on a bed of leeks with a tarragon and mustard seed sauce. Or you could indulge in an expensive rarity for these parts, Breton lobster with red wine butter and *zucchini*. For pudding, try the typically Austrian cream cheese dumpling with apricot mousse. Petits fours are served with the coffee.

~

TYPE OF FOOD international

OPENING TIMES evenings only, from 20.15; closed 15 Jan–15 Mar

CREDIT CARDS MC, V

PRICE €€€

IBIZA

SANTA EULARIA

NINA'S
~ COUNTRY RESTAURANT ~

Carrer Isidor Macabich 33, 07850 Santa Eularia
Tel 971 33 22 43

The eponymous Nina is the daughter of Nicole and Volker Schiemer, who sold their discothèque and bistro in Cologne to escape to the sun. On a visit to Santa Eularia, Nina fell in love with a little house by the sea housing a poorly-run restaurant, and persuaded her parents to reopen it in new attire. The reception room was painted in sunny colours and fitted out with contemporary furniture; and a chef, Wolfgang Brinkmann, was found to complete the picture. Santa Eularia is quietish spot, without much to offer in the way of restaurants, and Nina's fills the gap admirably, with good food – and great sea views as a bonus.

The menu, devised by Brinkmann and the owners, offers an excellent fish soup for a starter. Outstanding main course fish dishes include a salmon filet in saffron sauce, or baby turbot with caper butter. For a meat alternative, try the rack of lamb with herbs, potato wedges and butter beans. Expert cellar man Ralf Quodt has assembled an interesting collection of French, Spanish and German wines.

~

Type of food international

Opening times 19.00-24.00; closed Wed and Nov

Credit cards MC, V

Price €€€

IBIZA

SANT ANTONI

VILLA MERCEDES
Village restaurant

Passeig de la Mar s/n, 07820 Sant Antoni
Tel 971 34 85 43

The harbour town of Sant Antoni has a charm all its own, and nothing in common with Ibiza Town and its frenetic nightlife. Boatloads of sun-worshipping holidaymakers in search of secluded bathing beaches often drop anchor here opposite Villa Mercedes, which was formerly one of Sant Antoni's finest residences, and enjoys a prominent position.

The new owners have breathed new life into it, giving the interior a refined style – nothing flash here. The balconies on the upper floor provide a fine view of the harbour. Cocktails and aperitifs are served at the charming garden bar.

For starters, you are offered a fresh salad with marinated anchovies on a curd cheese and *confit* of tomatoes; *carpaccio* of tuna accompanied by a fine prawn mayonnaise; or the home-made duck liver paté. Main meat courses include pigeon in melon juice or leg of suckling pig with apple purée, both delicious. The choice of fish is enormous. The *serviola* with smoked bacon and a strong game sauce is outstanding. Spanish wines dominate the wine list. Not-exactly-slimming desserts are the crowning glory.

Type of food Spanish/international

Opening times daily, 20.00-24.00

Credit cards MC, V

Price €€-€€€

IBIZA

Sant Josep

VILLAGE
~ COUNTRY RESTAURANT ~

Calo d'en Real (Cala Vedella direction), 07830 Sant Josep
Tel 971 80 80 01

The fabulously situated Village is one of the most elegant restaurants on Ibiza, with its unique interior decoration and a certain unassuming class probably attributable to owner Roger Stohr. He knows how to mix superlative cocktails, and these are stylishly served to guests as they ponder the wonderful sunsets before applying themselves to chef Juan José's culinary masterpieces. (You are in the middle of nowhere here, with pine forest all around and with breathtaking views over the sea.)

As an entrée, a chilled cream of melon soup with fine shreds of Serrano ham is a delicious surprise; so, as a main course, is the *osso bucco* (with a wonderful sauce) or the *carpaccio* of spiced, tender beef.

There's a well-stocked cellar. Desserts are seductive, and you wind up in style with black coffee accompanied by a fine Cardenal de Mendoza, Juan Carlos I or a subtle Le Panto, all of which can claim to be Spain's best cognacs.

~

Type of food Spanish/international

Opening times 20.00-24.00; closed 1 Nov-20 Dec and 15 Feb-Easter

Credit cards MC, V

Price €€-€€€

Hotel & Restaurant Names
Hotels

A
Alcaufar Vell, Sant Lluis 96
Almirante Collingwood, Es Castell, Menorca 93

B
Hotel Bahia, Peguera, Mallorca 69
Hotel Bendinat, Portals Nous, Mallorca 74
Biniarrocca, Sant Lluis, Menorca 98
Biniatram, Cala Morell, Menorca 90
Binibona, Caimari, Mallorca 34
Binidali, Sant Lluis, Menorca 97
Born, Hotel, Palma, Mallorca 63

C
Ca'n Ai, Sóller, Mallorca 81
Ca'n Calco, Moscari, Mallorca 61
Ca'n Coll, Sóller, Mallorca 82
Ca'n Curreu, Santa Eularia, Ibiza 103
Cala Sant Vicenç, Pollença, Mallorca 71
Ca'n Furiós, Binibona, Mallorca 31
Ca'n Moragues, Art·, Mallorca 28
Ca'n Verdera, Fornalutx, Mallorca 54
Ca's Comte, Lloseta, Mallorca 55
Ca's Gasi, Santa Gertrudis, Ibiza 104
Ca's Pla, Sant Miguel, Ibiza 101
Ca's Puers, Sóller, Mallorca 83
Ca's Sant, Sóller, Mallorca 84
Casal Santa Eulalia, Santa Margalida, Mallorca 79

E
Ets Abellons, Caimari, Mallorca 35

F
Es Figueral Nou, Montuiri, Mallorca 60
Finca Barcelona, Buñola, Mallorca 33

H
Hacienda Na Xamena, Sant Miguel, Ibiza 102
L'Hermitage, Orient, Mallorca 62

J
Hotel Juma, Pollença, Mallorca 72

M
Mar I Vent, Banyulbufar, Mallorca 30
Mofarés, Calvia, Mallorca 39
Es Moli, Deià, Mallorca 48
Monaber Nou, Campanet, Mallorca 41

N
Los Naranjos, Son Termes, Mallorca 88
Hotel Niu, Cala Sant Vicent, Mallorca 38

O
Ocean Drive, Talamanca , Ibiza 99
S'Olivaret, Alaró, Mallorca 25

P
Palacio Casa Calesa, Palma, Mallorca 64
Pasarela, Mahó, Menorca 127
Hotel Patricia, Ciutadella, Menorca 91
Petit Cala Fornells, Peguera, Mallorca 36
Port Mahó, Mahó, Menorca 95
Posada d'es Moli, Es Pil-Lari-Sanfrancisco, Mallorca 49
La Posada del Marques, Esporles, Mallorca 51
Possessió Binicomprat, Algaida, Mallorca 26

R
Read's Hotel, Santa Maria, Malorca 80
Es Recó de Randa, Randa, Mallorca 77
La Reserva Rotana, Manacor, Mallorca 57
La Residencia, Deià, Mallorca 46

S
Sa Bassa Rotja, Porreres, Mallorca 73
Sa Galera, Ca's Concos, Mallorca 44
Sa Perdrissa, Deià, Mallorca 47
Sa Plana Petit Hotel, Estellencs, Mallorca 52
Sa Posada d'Aumallia, Felanitx, Mallorca 53
Sant Blai, Campos, Mallorca 42
Sant Ignasi, Ciutadella, Menorca 92
Sant Salvador, Art·, Mallorca 29
Scott's, Binissalem, Mallorca 32
S'Hostal d'Esporles, Esporles, Mallorca 50
Son Amoixa Vell, Manacor, Mallorca 58
Son Bernadinet, Campos, Mallorca 43
Son Bleda, Sóller, Mallorca 85
Son Esteve, Andratx , Mallorca 27
Son Jordà, Ruberts, Mallorca 78
Son Gener, Manacor, Mallorca 59
Son Malero, Calvia, Mallorca 40
Son Mola Vell, Son Macia, Mallorca 86
Son Net, Puigpuntent, Mallorca 76
Son Porró, Costitx, Mallorca 45
Son Sureda, Manacor, Mallorca 87
Son Triay Nou, Ferreries, Menorca 94
Son Xotana, Pina, Mallorca 70
Ses Rotges, Cala Rajada, Majorca 37

T

La Torre del Canónigo, Ibiza Town, Ibiza 100

V

Villa Italia, Port d'Andratx, Mallorca 75
Vistamar, Valdemosa, Mallorca 89

RESTAURANTS

B

La Bóveda I and II, Palma, Mallorca 113
El Brasero, Ibiza Town, Ibiza 131
El Bungalow, Ciutat Jardi, Mallorca 107

C

Café Balear, Ciutadella, Menorca 126
Cala Conills, Sant Telm, Mallorca 123
Ca'n Bernat, Sant Climent, Menorca 130
Ca's Puers, Sûller, Mallorca 125
Chopin, Palma, Mallorca 114
Colon, Portocolom, Mallorca 119
Hostal Corona, Palma-El-Terreno, Mallora 68
El Corsario, Ibiza Town, Ibiza 132

F

Flanigan, Puerto Portals, Mallorca 120

M

Meson Caín Torrat, Calvia, Mallorca 106
Mira Mar, Port d'Andratx, Mallorca 116

N

Na Burgesa, Genova, Mallorca 112
Nina's, Santa Eularia, Ibiza 133
Restaurant Bar Nou, Es Capdellá, Mallorca 110

P

Pasarela, Mahó, Menorca 127
El Patio, Port d'Andratx, Mallorca 117
Hotel Portixol, Palma, Mallorca 66
Portobello, Mahó, Mahó 128

R

Es Raco díes Teix, Deià, Mallorca 108
Los Rafaeles, Palma, Mallorca 115
Es Recó, Randa, Mallorca 122

S

Sa Font, Palma, Palma, Mallorca 65

Sa Tafona Son Net, Puigpuntent, Mallorca 121
Sa Vinya, Deià, Mallorca 109
San Lorenzo, Palma, Mallorca 67
La Sirena, Mahó, Menorca 129
Son Llarg, Estellencs, Mallorca 111
Restaurant Stay, Port de Pollença, Mallorca 118

T
La Tulipe, S'Arracó, Mallorca 124

V
Villa Mercedes, Sant Antoni, Ibiza 133
Village, Sant Josef, Ibiza 135

HOTEL LOCATIONS

A
Alaró, Mallorca, SíOlivaret 25
Algaida, Mallorca, Possessió Binicomprat 26
Andratx , Mallorca, Son Esteve 27
Artà·, Mallorca, Ca'n Moragues 28
Artà·, Mallorca, Sant Salvador 29

B
Banyulbufar, Mallorca, Mar I Vent 30
Binibona, Mallorca, Ca'n Furiós 31
Binissalem, Mallorca, Scott's 32
Buñola, Mallorca, Finca Barcelona 33

C
Caimari, Mallorca, Binibona 34
Caimari, Mallorca, Ets Abellons 35
Cala Morell, Menorca, Biniatram 90
Cala Rajada, Majorca, Ses Rotges 37
Cala Sant Vicenç, Mallorca, Hotel Niu 38
Calvia, Mallorca, Mofarés 39
Calvia, Mallorca, Son Malero 40
Campanet, Mallorca, Monaber Nou 41
Campos, Mallorca, Sant Blai 42
Campos, Mallorca, Son Bernadinet 43
Ca's Concos, Mallorca, Sa Galera 44
Ciutadella, Menorca, Hotel Patricia 91
Ciutadella, Menorca, Sant Ignasi 92
Costitx, Mallorca, Son Porró 45

D
Deià, Mallorca, Es Moli 48
Deià, Mallorca, La Residencia 46
Deià, Mallorca, Sa Perdrissa 47

E

Es Castell, Menorca, Almirante Collingwood 93
Es Pil·Lari-Sanfrancisco, Mallorca, Posada d'es Moli 49
Esporles, Mallorca, La Posada del Marques 51
Esporles, Mallorca, S'Hostal d'Esporles, 50
Estellencs, Mallorca, Sa Plana Petit Hotel 52

F

Felanitx, Mallorca, Sa Posada d'Aumallia 53
Ferreries, Menorca, Son Triay Nou 94
Fornalutx, Mallorca, Caín Verdera 54

I

Ibiza Town, Ibiza, La Torre del Canónigo 100

L

Lloseta, Mallorca, Ca's Comte 55

M

Mahó, Menorca, Pasarela 127
Mahó, Menorca, Port Mahó 95
Manacor, Mallorca, La Reserva Rotana 57
Manacor, Mallorca, Son Amoixa Vell 58
Manacor, Mallorca, Son Gener 59
Manacor, Mallorca, Son Sureda 87
Montuiri, Mallorca, Es Figueral Nou 60
Moscari, Mallorca, Ca'n Calco 61

O

Orient, Mallorca, L'Hermitage 62

P

Palma, Mallorca, Hotel Born 63
Palma, Mallorca, Palacio Casa Calesa 64
Peguera, Mallorca, Hotel Bahia 69
Peguera, Mallorca, Petit Cala Fornells 36
Pina, Mallorca, Son Xotana, 70
Pollença, Mallorca, Hotel Juma 72
Pollença, Mallorca, Cala Sant Vicenç 71
Porreres, Mallorca, Sa Bassa Rotja 73
Portals Nous, Mallorca, Hotel Bendinat 74
Port d'Andratx, Mallorca, Villa Italia 75
Puigpuntent, Mallorca, Son Net 76

R

Randa, Mallorca, Es Recó de Randa 77
Ruberts, Mallorca, Son Jordà 78

S

Sant Lluis, Menorca, Alcaufar Vell, 96

Sant Lluis, Menorca, Biniarrocca 98
Sant Lluis, Menorca, Binidali 97
Sant Miguel, Ibiza, Ca's Pla 101
Sant Miguel, Ibiza, Hacienda Na Xamena 102
Santa Eularia, Ibiza, Ca'n Curreu 103
Santa Gertrudis, Ibiza, Ca's Gasi 104
Santa Margalida, Mallorca, Casal Santa Eulalia 79
Santa Maria, Mallorca, Read's Hotel 80
Sóller, Mallorca, Ca'n Ai 81
Sóller, Mallorca, Ca'n Coll 82
Sóller, Mallorca, Ca's Puers 83
Sóller, Mallorca, Ca's Sant 84
Sóller, Mallorca, Son Bleda 85
Son Macia, Mallorca, Son Mola Vell 86
Son Termes, Mallorca, Los Naranjos 88

T
Talamanca, Ibiza, Ocean Drive 99

V
Valdemosa, Mallorca, Vistamar 89

Restaurant Locations

C
Calvia, Mallorca, Meson Ca'n Torrat 106
Ciutat Jardi, Mallorca, El Bungalow 107
Ciutadella, Menorca, Café Balear 126

D
Deià, Mallorca, Es Raco díes Teix 108
Deià, Mallorca, Sa Vinya 109

E
Es Capdellà, Mallorca, Restaurant Bar Nou 110
Estellencs, Mallorca, Son Llarg 111

G
Genova, Mallorca, Na Burgesa 112

I
Ibiza Town, Ibiza, El Brasero 131
Ibiza Town, Ibiza , El Corsario 132

M
Mahó, Menorca, Pasarela 127
Mahó, Menorca, Portobello 128
Mahó, Menorca, La Sirena 129

P

Palma, Mallorca, La Bóveda I and II 113
Palma, Mallorca, Chopin 114
Palma, Mallorca, Hotel Portixol 66
Palma, Mallorca, Los Rafaeles 115
Palma, Mallorca, Sa Font 65
Palma, Mallorca, San Lorenzo 67
Palma-El-Terreno, Mallorca, Hostal Corona 68
Port d'Andratx, Mallorca, Mira Mar 116
Port d'Andratx, Mallorca, El Patio 117
Port de Pollença, Mallorca, Restaurant Stay 118
Portocolom, Mallorca, Colon 119
Puerto Portals, Mallorca, Flanigan 120
Puigpuntent, Mallorca, Sa Tafona Son Net 121

R

Randa, Mallorca, Es Recó 122

S

Sant Antoni, Ibiza, Villa Mercedes 133
Sant Climent, Menorca, Ca'n Bernat 130
Santa Eularia, Ibiza, Nina's 133
Sant Josef, Ibiza, Village 135
Sant Telm, Mallorca, Cala Conills 123
S'Arracó, Mallorca, La Tulipe 124
Sóller, Mallorca, Ca's Puers 125

SPECIAL OFFERS

Buy your *Charming Small Hotel Guide* by post directly from the publisher and you'll get a worthwhile discount. *

Titles available:	Retail price	Discount price
Austria	£9.99	£8.50
Britain	£10.99	£9.50
Britain's Most Distinctive Bed & Breakfasts	£9.99	£8.50
France	£11.99	£10.50
France: Bed & Breakfast	£9.99	£8.50
Germany	£9.99	£8.50
Greece	£10.99	£9.50
Ireland	£9.99	£8.50
Italy	£11.99	£10.50
Paris	£10.99	£9.50
Southern France	£10.99	£9.50
Spain	£9.99	£8.50
Switzerland	£9.99	£8.50
Tuscany & Umbria	£9.99	£8.50
USA: Florida	£9.99	£8.50
USA: New England	£9.99	£8.50
Venice and North-East Italy	£9.99	£8.50

Please send your order to:
   Book Sales,
   Duncan Petersen Publishing Ltd,
   31 Ceylon Road, London W14 OPY
enclosing: 1) the title you require and number of copies
   2) your name and address
   3) your cheque made out to:
   Duncan Petersen Publishing Ltd
*Offer applies to this edition and to UK only.

VISIT DUNCAN PETERSEN'S TRAVEL WEBSITE AT
www.charmingsmallhotels.co.uk
• Research interesting places to stay • Online book ordering –special discounts • Room booking service

SPECIAL OFFERS

If you like *Charming Small Hotel Guides* you'll also enjoy Duncan Petersen's *Versatile Guides/Travel Planner & Guides*: outstanding all-purpose travel guides written by authors, not by committee.

Titles available:	Retail price	Discount price
Australia Travel Planner & Guide	£12.99	£10.50
California The Versatile Guide	£12.99	£10.50
Central Italy The Versatile Guide	£12.99	£10.50
England & Wales Walks Planner & Guide	£12.99	£10.50
Florida Travel Planner & Guide	£12.99	£10.50
France Travel Planner & Guide	£12.99	£10.50
Greece The Versatile Guide	£12.99	£10.50
Italy Travel Planner & Guide	£12.99	£10.50
Spain The Versatile Guide	£12.99	£10.50
Thailand The Versatile Guide	£12.99	£10.50
Turkey The Versatile Guide	£12.99	£10.50

Travelling by car? Duncan Petersen's *Backroads* driving guides include original routes and tours – avoid the motorways and main roads and explore the real country. Full colour easy to read mapping; recommended restaurants and local specialities; practical advice on where to stop, visit and picnic.

Titles available:	Retail price	Discount price
Britain on Backroads	£9.99	£8.50
France on Backroads	£9.99	£8.50
Italy on Backroads	£9.99	£8.50
Spain on Backroads	£9.99	£8.50

Please send your order to:
    Book Sales,
    Duncan Petersen Publishing Ltd,
    31 Ceylon Road, London W14 OPY
    enclosing: 1) title you require and number of copies
                    2) your name and address
                    3) your cheque made out to:
         Duncan Petersen Publishing Ltd
*Offer applies applies to this edition and to UK only.